Spanish Phonology and Morphology:
A Generative View

William W. Cressey

Georgetown University Press, Washington, D.C. 20057

Library of Congress Cataloging in Publication Data

Cressey, William W
    Spanish phonology and morphology.

    Bibliography: p.
    Includes index.
    1. Spanish language--Phonology. 2. Spanish
language--Grammar, Generative. I. Title.
PC4131.C7   461'.5   78-23327
ISBN 0-87840-045-1

International Standard Book Number: 0-87840-045-1

FOR GINA, SALLY, AND JAMES

CONTENTS

FOREWORD

This book is intended as an introduction both to the formal study of Spanish phonology and to the framework of generative phonology. The analysis of Spanish is presented in terms of an extended version of the theoretical framework set forth in Chomsky and Halle (1968) The Sound Pattern of English.

Work on Spanish phonology within the generative framework began essentially with two MIT dissertations: Foley (1965) and Harris (1969). The latter of these was published as an MIT monograph and Harris subsequently published numerous papers on Spanish phonology. Harris' work thus constitutes an important foundation for what is presented in this book.

I have also included revised versions of some analyses of my own which were originally presented in journal articles and papers read at conferences and symposia.

The most controversial issue of phonology as of this writing is perhaps the question of abstractness. Just how abstract an underlying representation can one accept as a plausible hypothesis concerning the competence of native speakers? In an attempt to develop a new point of view concerning this issue, I have subdivided the rules which describe the sound system of Spanish into groups according to the formal properties of the rules themselves. Unlike previous generative treatments, this book recognizes specific subcomponents containing the following types of rules: Detail Rules (Chapter One), Low Level Allophonic Process Rules (Chapter Three), Word-level Phonology Rules (Chapter Four), Everywhere Rules (Chapter Five), and Inflectional Morphology Rules (Chapter Six). In general terms, the more abstract rules are taken up in the later chapters of the book. Contrary to the expectation expressed in Anderson (1974:xv), I have not encountered situations in Spanish which require that the rules of the various components be inter-mixed. The main advantage of this division is that it makes it possible to assume that different speakers control the sound system in different ways. Specifically, I assume that some speakers remember vocabulary items in terms of rather abstract

representations, whereas other speakers remember more concrete
versions of these same words. In effect, this assumption constitutes a compromise of sorts between advocates of abstract phonology and advocates of more concrete phonology. The details
of this variable view of abstraction are set forth in Section 2.9.

ACKNOWLEDGMENTS

I should like to acknowledge assistance of various sorts. My research has been supported, in part, by the American Council of Learned Societies and by the Georgetown University Faculty Fellowship Program. Free use of computer time has been made available to me by the Central Computer Facility at Georgetown University. Many of the rules presented here have been tested and refined by using a phonological grammar testing program made available to me by Joyce Friedman together with a complete lexicon of Spanish which was prepared initially by Fred Stahl and Gary Scavnicky.

In addition, for many helpful comments, corrections, suggestions, for help with computational problems, and for insights, encouragement, and many other types of assistance, I should like to extend thanks to all of the following: Cathy Adkins, James Alatis, Joe Campbell, Nick Centola, Gina Cressey, Carroll Davis, Mary Ellen Garcia, Donna Gleason, Giuliano Gnugnoli, Carol Greenberg, Jorge Guitart, Deanna Hammond, James Harris, Eric Heinz, Joan Hooper, Sue Izzo, Keith Krause, Charles Kreidler, Robert Lado, Jan Larsen, Jim McConnel, Frank 'Bro' Mullen, Richard J. O'Brien, S.J., Gino Parisi, Penny Pinny, Solomon I. Sara, S.J., Lisa Sulski, Steve Vann, Delia Villarroel, Norm Waite, Elliot Woodaman, and Janet Ziegler.

0. INTRODUCTION

0.0 Introduction. This book deals with the sound system of Spanish. The topics discussed range from a quite detailed and concrete phonetic description of Spanish sounds to a rather abstract and speculative analysis of certain classes of irregular verbs.

The theoretical basis for the analyses presented is the theory of generative grammar, developed originally by Noam Chomsky, of MIT, and others in the early 1950s. Since there exists considerable disagreement among proponents of this school of linguistics concerning rather fundamental questions of linguistic theory, I have attempted to outline in this introduction the basic theoretical assumptions which underlie the analyses presented in this book. The major ingredients of the framework can be explained in terms of the answers to some fundamental questions concerning the research program to be followed (Section 0.1), the enunciation of two basic assumptions concerning the nature of language (Section 0.2), a commitment to particular goals (Section 0.3), the establishment of a method of evaluating the success of linguistic research (Section 0.4), and finally, the subdivision of linguistic research into subfields (Section 0.5).

0.1 Preliminary questions concerning the research program. A research program can be thought of as a decision to investigate the properties of something using a particular methodology. The research leads to the formulation of hypotheses based upon the available evidence and upon the theoretical framework selected by the researcher. The following sections explain the positions taken in this book regarding some aspects of the research program.

0.1.1 The object of analysis. What constitutes the entity described by a linguistic analysis? Of course, in general terms, the object of analysis is, by definition, a language or perhaps certain aspects of a language. A complete linguistic analysis

1

of a given language (a grammar of that language) can be defined as a set of rules which express generalizations and restrictions about that language. But what constitutes the 'language'? In what medium do these generalizations and restrictions exist?

This question arises in connection with most work in linguistics, and it has been answered in a number of ways.

(1) It is possible to maintain that what is to be analyzed is actual utterances of the language in question as recorded on tape or as transcribed in phonetic notation. The analysis consists of the formulation of all and only those generalizations which are supported by the recorded data. One who attempts an analysis of this sort is analyzing performances. This is a very concrete position, and is the position adopted, for the most part, by the American structuralists.

(2) At the opposite end of the abstractness spectrum is the point of view that the linguist is analyzing the language itself, independently of how it is used by speakers. This type of analysis is carried out by formulating a set of rules which express all the generalizations and restrictions which the analyst can find in the language. This is the point of view, for the most part, of the classical grammarians.

(3) Generative grammar has adopted an intermediate position. Generative grammarians attempt to characterize human linguistic competence. Unlike position (2), the generative position does not treat language as an entity which is independent of speakers. Generative analysis must express generalizations and restrictions which native speakers are capable of grasping. Unlike position (1), the study of competence does not depend upon actual recorded utterances. The linguist assumes that native speakers actually produce many utterances which are incorrect (ungrammatical) according to the subconscious rules which the speakers have internalized. For example, speakers make slips of the tongue, change gears in mid sentence, and insert all sorts of stall words such as uh, etc. These phenomena, according to the generative linguist, are performance phenomena, and are outside the domain of grammar. Each native speaker knows, subconsciously, the rules of his language and can usually tell the linguist whether any given sentence is correct or incorrect.

The formulation of an explicit set of rules which characterizes what the native speaker subconsciously knows about his language constitutes, as I have said, the investigation of competence. However, since the generalizations and restrictions actually controlled by individual speakers vary from person to person, it is necessary to take the definition of competence one step further. The object of analysis is not the competence of any one particular speaker of a language but rather the competence of an idealized speaker of that language--that is, a hypothetical speaker who controls his language in the most efficient way possible, a native speaker who formulates as many generalizations as can be extracted from the data available to him.

The generative position, then, is that the task of linguistic analysis is the formulation of all and only those generalizations which are possible and plausible rules available for use by native speakers. This is the approach which is followed in this book.

0.1.2 Research procedures and evidence. Since human linguistic competence is not directly observable, what procedures can be used to obtain information as to its nature? What can be considered evidence in favor of the hypothesis that some particular generalization is a valid part of the competence of the idealized speaker? This question must be taken up in two parts.

First, there is the question of determining what is correct and what is incorrect usage. Generative grammarians have used tape recordings of utterances in order to make this determination, but they do not feel bound by the recordings. If a native speaker says something which is consistently rejected by other native speakers, then that utterance is considered either deviant or a performance error, and its properties are not considered to be part of competence. Thus, the intuitions of native speakers, their judgments concerning utterances which are presented to them, also constitute important data to be investigated.

In this treatment of Spanish phonology, I have accepted the raw phonetic data presented in Navarro Tomás (1968) as largely correct. In addition, I have used tape recorded material of various sorts, anatomical sketches, and the judgments of native speakers whom I have consulted.

The second part of the question has to do with the analysis. Once the observable facts have been established, how does one investigate the generalizations and restrictions which are presumed to underlie those facts? What types of observable phenomena can be accepted as support for an abstract nonobservable hypothesis? To cite a specific example, what justification can be given in support of the hypothesis that a particular word is represented in some particular way in the minds of native speakers? In this case, as well, a number of answers have been given. First, in order to be a possible analysis, the proposed underlying representation must yield the correct results when the rules of pronunciation proposed along with it, are applied to it. After this crucial test is passed, it is necessary to show that the analysis is not simply possible, but also plausible. In support of their analyses, linguists have offered evidence of the following sorts. (1) Forms which existed in earlier stages of the language under consideration, and which exhibit phonetically the essential properties of the proposed analysis may be used as evidence. (2) Forms which exist in other related dialects or languages, and substandard forms may be used as evidence. (3) Forms which are related to the word in question and which are presumed to derive from the same root may be used as evidence. For example, if the underlying form /nokte/ is proposed for [noče] noche 'night (noun)', the linguist may cite the related word [nokturno] nocturno 'night (adj)' as evidence in favor of his representation /nokte/, since nocturno contains the [kt] cluster phonetically. (This analysis is discussed in detail in Sections 4.3.1.3 and 4.8.) (4) How native speakers deal with loan words, nonsense words, and foreign languages can also be adduced as evidence in order to gain some insight into the rules which the native speakers possess. For example, the fact that a native speaker of Spanish will frequently produce [æn estrít] for English a street can be considered as evidence in support of the hypothesis that the grammar of Spanish includes a rule which adds epenthetic [e] to words such as estación, español, escuela, which are represented in the mind without the initial [e]. (This analysis is discussed in detail in Section 4.1.4.)

In this book, neither forms which existed in earlier stages of Spanish nor forms which exist in other dialects are considered evidence in support of any analysis. The best evidence, in my view, is to be extracted from the physical forms themselves. The types of evidence described in (3) and (4) are considered valid support for an underlying form which cannot be deduced directly from the phonetic form of the item in question; however, these types of evidence can only be accepted tentatively. I take the position that in any particular instance the burden of proof weighs more heavily upon that analysis which differs more from the physical form of an item than upon that analysis which differs less from the particular form in question.

0.1.3 Theoretical basis for the analysis. What overall theory of language serves as the basis for the specific hypotheses proposed by the investigator? More specifically, how do the various aspects of language (meaning, form, and sound) relate to each other; and how is the vocabulary of a language related to its overall structure? What constraints on the nature of possible rules are believed to characterize natural language in general and differentiate it from other organizational systems?

The answers to these questions are much more complex than the answers to the questions discussed in Sections 0.1.1 and 0.1.2. In general terms, it can be said that generative grammar depends upon the tenet that native speakers are able to control the patterns of their language in terms of rules and generalizations which are considerably more abstract than those which were proposed by some previous theories, most notably, American structural linguistics. Considerably more details about both generative grammar in general and the particular version of generative grammar which serves as the basis for this book are mentioned as specific issues arise. The remaining sections of this Introduction deal with the theoretical framework of generative grammar in general. The theory of phonology is discussed in Chapter Two and theoretical refinements are

introduced throughout the text, particularly at the beginning
and end of each chapter.

0.2 Assumptions concerning the nature of language. There
are two important assumptions concerning the nature of human
linguistic competence which distinguish generative grammar from
other approaches.

0.2.1 Rule-governed creativity. Perhaps the most important
difference between generative grammar and previous theories
is embodied in the definition of language as rule-governed creativity. The word 'creativity' in this context is intended as a
denial of the earlier assumption that language is based upon
habit. Thus, the term 'rule-governed creativity' implies that
when someone produces an utterance, he is not simply repeat-
ing, by force of habit, one of a large set of sentences which
he has stored in his memory, but rather he is creating that
utterance spontaneously by combining the words that he knows,
according to certain principles which he also knows. These
principles constitute the rule-governed aspect of language and
are essentially the grammatical rules of the language in question.
   It must be made clear that the word 'knows' has been used in
two distinct ways in the preceding paragraph. When it is
claimed that a native speaker 'knows' the words of his language, this is similar to what we mean when we say that a
person 'knows' the capitals of all the states. That is, he has
all the words stored in his memory, and he can produce the desired words when he needs to use them. However, the claim
that a native speaker 'knows' the rules of the language means
something quite different. This type of 'knowing' is more similar to what is meant by saying that someone 'knows' how to
ride a bicycle. In general, people who have not studied formal
grammar are not able to discuss or recite the grammar rules of
their own languages. However, they do have a working knowledge of those rules, as evidenced by the fact that they are
able to recognize and produce correct sentences.

0.2.2 Infinite use of finite means. Related to the assumption
discussed in Section 0.2.1 is the assumption that the competence
of a speaker of a language enables him to make infinite use of
the finite items which comprise the vocabulary of that language.
Since sentences can be incorporated into other sentences as de-
pendent clauses, the combinatory potential of a language is
theoretically infinite. A good example of this can be seen in
the poem The house that Jack built. Each new verse of this
poem is constructed by adding a new main clause at the beginning of the preceding verse. (For example, verse (1): This
is the house that Jack built; verse (2): This is the malt that
lay in the house that Jack built; verse (3): This is the rat
that ate the malt that lay in the house that Jack built, etc.,

etc.) The poem is thus a potentially never ending series of sentences containing relative clauses. Eventually, a verse will be constructed which is difficult to recite because of its length; however, it will still be completely comprehensible and grammatically correct. From the infinite potential of language, it follows that it would be impossible to construct a complete list of all the acceptable utterances of a language. It also follows that an individual native speaker is capable of producing and understanding sentences which he has never heard before. Generative grammarians take this fact as proof of the claim that language use is based upon rule-governed creativity, rather than upon habit.

0.3 **The goals of linguistic research.** The major goal of linguistic research, according to generative grammarians, is the investigation of the human linguistic capabilities discussed in the preceding section. The linguist is interested in the nature of this ability to construct new utterances which are grammatical, and in how this ability is acquired by the language learner. Some of the specific questions to be answered are the following: How may linguistic ability best be characterized? Which aspects of linguistic ability, if any, are innate, and which are acquired by a learning process? What properties are shared by all languages? How may the principles or rules of a specific language best be described?

In the course of this investigation, two primary research activities are carried out more or less simultaneously and interdependently.

0.3.1 **Analysis of particular languages.** Linguists attempt to work out generative grammars or, more typically, segments of grammars, for languages with which they are relatively familiar.

0.3.2 **Analysis of the phenomenon of language in general.** As the linguist analyzes a particular language, he also contributes to our understanding of language in general. This contribution is accomplished by proposing refinements in the theoretical framework within which he is working. The theoretical framework consists of such elements as the following: constraints restricting the types of rules which may be written, notational devices which may be used in order to combine two or more partially similar and related rules into one statement, systems for computing the complexity of a given rule and comparing it to an alternative rule in order to determine which statement is less complex, and conventions governing the ways in which rules may be written and are to be interpreted.

The theoretical framework expresses what the linguist claims to have learned about natural language in general. Therefore each theoretical element must be supported by evidence from specific languages.

0.4 Evaluation of linguistic analyses. In order to evaluate opposing hypotheses, both concerning specific languages and concerning the general provisions of the theoretical framework, it is necessary to develop a principled way of measuring the success of an analysis or of a theory. Within the generative framework, evaluations of this sort are usually carried out in terms of what Chomsky (1964) called three levels of adequacy. The first two levels of adequacy serve to evaluate grammars of particular languages and the third serves to evaluate the theoretical framework.

0.4.1 Observational adequacy. A grammar of a specific language is said to meet observational adequacy if it defines all and only the grammatical sentences of that language, each sentence associated with its correct pronunciation, or pronunciations, and its true meaning or meanings. This is the lowest level of adequacy and is the first requirement that must be met before a particular grammar can be considered as a hypothesis concerning the language in question. Nothing is required at this level of adequacy regarding the appropriateness of the generalizations entailed by the rules; it is only required that the rules predict the actual pronunciations and meanings of all grammatical sentences and rule out all ungrammatical sentences. If a grammatical statement predicts ungrammatical sentences, specifies the wrong meaning, or yields the wrong pronunciation of any utterance, then that grammatical statement fails to meet observational adequacy. To take a specific example from Spanish phonology, a grammar containing a rule which voices /s/ before all voiced obstruents (which is correct) but also before /p/, /t/, and /k/ (which is incorrect) fails to meet observational adequacy. This rule would specify the wrong pronunciation, e.g. *[ezte] for [este] <u>este</u> 'this'.

0.4.2 Descriptive adequacy. A grammar of a specific language is said to meet descriptive adequacy if, in addition to meeting observational adequacy, its rules express the relevant generalizations in terms of which the native speakers of that language control the structures and forms of the language. Thus, as observational adequacy is related to a physical reality, so descriptive adequacy is related to a psychological reality; a grammar meets descriptive adequacy if its rules are psychologically real. Since psychological reality is not an observable phenomenon, it is considerably more difficult to measure descriptive adequacy than it is to measure observational adequacy. In most cases, judgments of descriptive adequacy must be expressed in terms of the idealized speaker who controls his language in the most efficient way possible (see Section 0.1.1).

0.4.3 Explanatory adequacy. This is the highest level of adequacy, and it applies not to individual grammars, but to the theoretical framework itself. A theoretical framework achieves explanatory adequacy when a mechanical method of measuring simplicity is included in the framework, and when simplicity as measured mechanically corresponds to descriptive adequacy. That is, a theoretical framework achieves explanatory adequacy to the extent that it formally characterizes the notion of an optimally efficient system available to native speakers of a language.

0.5 The organization of a generative grammar. A generative grammar describes form, meaning, and sound. The grammar consists of a series of 'generative' rules, each one of which is a statement to the effect that a certain linguistic unit X is also to be considered an instance of a certain other linguistic unit Y. Generally speaking, each rule can be viewed as an instruction to rewrite a given input so that it conforms to what is specified in the output. The specific form of phonological rules is discussed in detail in Section 2.4. For the general purposes of this introduction, however, let us consider a very traditional first rule of a syntactic component. Rule (0.1) states that 'every instance of the symbol S, which stands for "sentence", is to be expanded into the string NP (noun phrase) followed by VP (verb phrase)'.

(0.1)   S → NP   VP

The symbol S is the starting point of the entire grammar, and other instances of S occur inside main sentences as subordinate clauses. Each time Rule (0.1) applies to an S node, the result is the partial diagram shown in Figure 0.1.

Figure 0.1.   Partial tree generated by Rule 0.1.

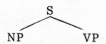

Subsequent rules then specify the internal structure of noun phrases and of verb phrases and of the many other types of constituents which make up sentences. Later rules modify the word order of some sentences (for example, to form the passive El ladrón fue atrapado por la policía 'The thief was trapped by the police' from the active La policía atrapó al ladrón 'The police trapped the thief'). In addition to rules which specify syntactic structure, there are rules which add vocabulary items to sentences, rules which specify the meanings of sentences, and rules which specify the pronunciations of sentences.

All of these rules taken together can be said to 'generate' (i.e. specify) all and only the correct sentences of a language and associate with each sentence its correct pronunciations and true meanings. Thus, a grammar of this sort is called a 'generative' grammar.

Generative grammars are usually divided into components.   A syntactic component describes sentence structure, a semantic component describes meaning, a phonological component describes pronunciation, and a lexical component describes the vocabulary. Since the late 1960s, there have been several alternative proposals concerning the relationship between syntax, semantics, and the lexicon.   It is generally agreed, however, that the phonological component operates upon the output of the syntax and the lexicon, and therefore, the disagreements which exist have little or no bearing upon how the phonological component is related to the rest of the grammar.   In Figure 0.2, I present a schematic diagram of a generative grammar which shows how the grammar relates the pronunciation of a sentence to its meaning, but the particular model which I have diagrammed here does not take any particular stand as to the internal organization of the syntax-semantics-lexicon portion of the grammar.   Figure 0.1 views the speaker as beginning at the top of the diagram, with an idea which he encodes into a sound stream, and views the hearer as beginning at the bottom of the diagram with a sound stream which he decodes into an idea.

Figure 0.2.   The organization of a generative grammar.

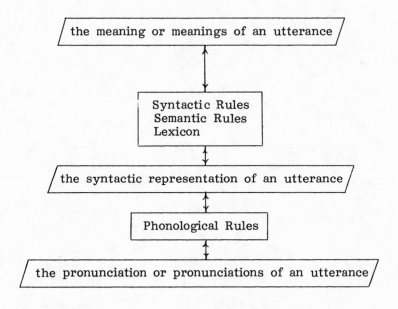

The phonological component relates a syntactic representation of an utterance to the systematic phonetic representation of that same utterance.   The syntactic representation which serves as the input to the phonological component consists of a string of lexical units, each one represented in a manner analogous to the way a speaker might store that particular word in his memory. The phonetic representation, which is the output of the phonological component, is the speaker-hearer's conception of the phonetic properties of that same utterance.

The internal organization of the phonological component is discussed in Section 2.8. We turn now to an examination of the most concrete representation of utterances: the systematic phonetic representation.

CHAPTER 1

DISTINCTIVE FEATURE CLASSIFICATION
OF THE SOUNDS OF SPANISH

1.0 Introduction. In this chapter, the sounds of Spanish
are described and classified according to a system of distinctive features. The classification system used here differs somewhat from the International Phonetic Association (IPA) classification system, which forms the basis for most phonetic description undertaken by autonomous phonemicists. However, an
application of the IPA system to the sounds of Spanish (as
illustrated in Figure 1.1) serves as a convenient starting place.
An explanation of the IPA terminology and a description of each
of the sounds of Spanish is presented in the Appendix. For
more detailed discussions, see IPA (1949) and Navarro Tomás
(1968).

1.1 Phonetic description in a generative grammar. Phonetic
description in a generative grammar differs from an IPA description in three important ways. First, the phonetic representation
in a generative grammar describes a mental reality, not a physical one (Section 1.1.1); second, a system of features, each of
which describes a property of speech sounds, replaces the IPA
classification system (Section 1.1.2); and third, two levels of
phonetic representation ('broad' and 'narrow' phonetic representations) are distinguished (Section 1.1.3).

1.1.1 Systematic phonetic representations. The first important difference between phonetics as envisioned by generative
phonologists and by phoneticians is that a generative phonetic
representation describes a mental reality, not a physical one.
Traditionally, phoneticians have attempted to describe the physical speech signal itself. However, the most concrete level of
description in a generative phonology (called the 'systematic
phonetic level') is, like all other levels of a generative grammar,
a representation of linguistic competence. Thus, the systematic

11

Figure 1.1. IPA system of classification as applied to the principal sounds of Spanish.

	bilabial	labio-dental	inter-dental	dental	alveolar	palato-alveolar	palatal	velar
stops	p b			t d				k g
fricatives	ƀ	f	θ z	đ			y	x gʷ
affricates						ĉ	ŷ	
sibilants				ş z̧		s z		
nasals	m	m̧	ņ	ņ	n	ñ	ñ	ŋ
laterals			ḽ	ḽ	l	ḽ	ĩ	
flaps					r			
trills					r̃			
glides							j	w
vowels							i u į ų e o ę ǫ ä å a	

phonetic representation describes a speaker's conception of the
speech signal, rather than the speech signal itself. The speaker's conception of the speech signal has been defined as '...
part of a theory about the instructions sent from the central
nervous system to the speech apparatus' (Postal 1968:6); and
also as a perceptual reality, 'not a direct record of the speech
signal, but rather a representation of what the speaker of a
language takes to be the phonetic properties of an utterance'
(Chomsky and Halle 1968:295). This work (The sound pattern
of English) is the most comprehensive treatment both of generative phonological theory and of English phonology which has been
published to date. As it is referred to so often, it is referenced
simply as SPE.

This mental reality--the speaker's conception of the speech
signal--may or may not best be characterized in terms of distinctions which are present in the speech signal itself. Since
the speech signal is directly observable and is measurable with
laboratory equipment, it provides the best source of information
concerning the mental reality to be described by systematic
phonetic representations. Therefore, the strongest evidence in
favor of a particular systematic phonetic representation is demon-
strable identity to the speech signal. It is theoretically possible, however, that the mental reality makes distinctions which
are not measurable in the speech signal and/or ignores some of
the distinctions which are measurable. Naturally, anyone who
proposes a systematic phonetic representation which differs from
the physical signal, must provide evidence which supports his
representation.

1.1.2 **Distinctive features as the basic units of phonetic
description.** In the IPA classification of sounds, each sound is
characterized by specifying point of articulation, manner of
articulation, and whether or not the sound is voiced. The distinctive features system used in generative analyses is essentially an extension of this procedure. However, each distinctive
feature represents a single articulatory property of a sound,
whereas some of the IPA terms refer to more than a single
property each. For example, consider the following points of
articulation and the articulators which form the primary obstruction at each point:

bilabial: lips,
labio-dental: lip and teeth,
dental: tip of the tongue and teeth,
alveolar: tip of the tongue and gums,
palato-alveolar: tip of the tongue and palate,
palatal: body of the tongue and palate,
velar: body of the tongue and velum.

Since the various articulators are each mentioned in connection with two or more points of articulation, the articulators
themselves might be considered the primary elements in the

phonetic system, and the points of articulation might be characterized in terms of these articulators. In Figure 1.2, each point of articulation is characterized by a column of pluses and minuses, each of which indicates whether or not the articulator to the left contributes to the primary obstruction of sounds at that point of articulation.

Figure 1.2. Articulators used at each point of articulation.

	bilabial	labio-dental	dental	alveolar	palato-alveolar	palatal	velar
lips	+	+	-	-	-	-	-
teeth	-	+	+	-	-	-	-
gums	-	-	-	+	+	-	-
palate	-	-	-	-	+	+	-
tongue	-	-	+	+	+	+	+

Similarly, some of IPA designations for manners of articulation might be characterized in terms of the types of aperture involved in each, as shown in Figure 1.3.

Figure 1.3. Elements involved in certain manners of articulation.

	stops	fricatives	affricates
occlusion	+	-	+
friction	-	+	+

In a generative presentation, each sound is described in terms of a plus or minus (or sometimes, numerical) value for each of a set of distinctive features. Each distinctive feature describes a characteristic which is either present or absent in the articulation of the particular sound. For example, a sound marked [+ voiced] is produced with vocal cords vibrating, a sound marked [- voiced] is produced without vocal cords vibrating. All of the features, whether related to point of articulation or manner of articulation (including [voiced]), are included in a single list.

Thus the features suggested in Figures 1.2 and 1.3 might be combined in order to yield the partial matrix of Spanish consonants shown in Figure 1.4. In a matrix of this sort, the sounds of the language are listed across the top, the features are listed down the left of the chart, then the entire matrix is filled in with pluses, minuses, and sometimes numbers. Each sound is described by the column of feature specifications which appears beneath it.

Figure 1.4. Partial chart of Spanish consonants illustrating use of features.

	p	t	ĉ	k	b	d	ŷ	g	f	θ	s	x	ƀ	đ	y	ǥ	ǥʷ
lips	+	−	−	−	+	−	−	−	+	−	−	−	+	−	−	−	+
teeth	−	+	−	−	−	+	−	−	+	+	−	−	−	+	−	−	−
palate	−	−	+	−	−	−	+	−	−	−	+	−	−	−	+	−	−
velum	−	−	−	+	−	−	−	+	−	−	−	+	−	−	−	+	+
tongue	−	+	+	+	−	+	+	+	−	+	+	+	−	+	+	+	+
occlusion	+	+	+	+	+	+	+	+	−	−	−	−	−	−	−	−	−
friction	−	−	+	−	−	−	+	−	+	+	+	+	+	+	+	+	+
voice	−	−	−	−	+	+	+	+	−	−	−	−	−	+	+	+	+

In order to classify completely the sounds of a given language, a set of features must be aptly chosen so that no two sounds have the same specifications for all the features in the set.

The feature complexes used in Figures 1.2 and 1.4 are intended only as an illustration of how the system works. In practice, most features used in generative phonological analyses are less similar to the IPA terminology and are not so directly related to the articulators themselves. The particular set of features used throughout this book is based, in large part, upon the set of features defined in SPE. The features used in this analysis of Spanish are defined and explained in Section 1.2.

1.1.3 Narrow versus broad phonetic representations. In Section 1.1.2, reference is made to plus and minus specifications and, in addition, to numerical specifications for some features. Although the use of two types of feature specification might seem cumbersome at first, there is an important reason for allowing the use of both types of specification. When all the languages of the world are taken into account, the total number of sounds which are phonetically distinct from each other is extremely large. Distinct representations of each of these sounds must be provided at the phonetic level. However, the exclusive use of plus and minus values of features to accomplish these representations would entail the postulation of an unworkable number of distinctive features. Therefore, in order to accomplish the description of every minute phonetic difference which exists, numerical values for some features are specified by rules called 'Detail Rules' (see Postal 1964).

For example, a language having four vowel heights phonetically, but only three phonemic vowel heights, might be characterized as follows: the three vowel heights are distinguished at the phonemic level by using plus and minus values for the features [high] and [low] as shown in Figure 1.5. Detail Rules

Figure 1.5. Three phonemic vowel heights described using plus and minus values of two features.

	i	e	a
[high]	+	–	–
[low]	–	–	+

(1.1) through (1.3) then establish the four narrow phonetic heights shown in Figure 1.6 by marking the vowels [∅ high], [1 high], [2 high], and [3 high].

Figure 1.6. Four vowel heights at the narrow phonetic level described using numerical values of the feature [high].

	i	e	ę	a
[high]	3	2	1	0
[low]	–	–	–	+

(1.1)   [+ high] → [3 high]

(1.2)   [+ low] → [∅ high]

(1.3) $\begin{bmatrix} - \text{ high} \\ - \text{ low} \end{bmatrix} \rightarrow \begin{cases} [1 \text{ high}] \text{ in some specified environment} \\ [2 \text{ high}] \text{ elsewhere} \end{cases}$

In this study, two levels of phonetic representation are used.[1] The 'broad' phonetic representation consists exclusively of plus and minus specifications for the features, whereas the 'narrow' phonetic representation includes numerical values for some features which have been specified by Detail Rules. The narrow phonetic representation is therefore the most explicit and detailed representation of each segment.

1.2 **The set of distinctive features used in this study and their application to Spanish.** One of the ultimate goals of generative research is a feature system (i.e. a set of features and their definitions) which is suitable for the description of all languages. In practice, however, linguists have worked out differing feature systems designed to fit the needs of particular languages, presumably in the hope that successive refinements of the feature system made when taking account of more and more languages will point the way to a more correct set of features valid for all languages.

As explained in Section 0.3, work on particular languages and the refinement of the theoretical framework progresses hand in hand. Therefore, if a modification of the feature system is proposed in order to improve the description of a particular language, e.g. Spanish, the modification must also take into account the needs of languages which have been analyzed using the original system, for example, the analysis of English presented in SPE.

The set of distinctive features to be used in this study is, for the most part, the system used in SPE. However, some modifications of the SPE system are proposed in order to improve the description of Spanish.

1.2.1 The major classes. A convenient starting point in the classification of sounds is the division of speech sounds into broad categories similar to the familiar 'vowel' versus 'consonant' distinction. However, most linguistic studies have divided sounds into four basic categories rather than two:

Vowels:	i, e, a, o, u
Glides:	j, w
Liquids:	l and r type sounds
Consonants:	p, f, c, s, n, etc.

In SPE, this distinction was refined somewhat to include nasals and liquids in a single category called 'sonorant consonants', which are discussed more fully in Section 1.2.1.1.3.

Vowels:	i, e, a, o, u
Glides:	j, w
Sonorant consonants:	liquids and nasals
Obstruents:	all other consonants

1.2.1.1 Features which define the major classes. The four major classes are defined by the following features.

1.2.1.1.1 Syllabic [syl]. A sound which forms the nucleus of a syllable is syllabic [+ syl]; all other sounds are nonsyllabic [- syl].

In Spanish, only vowels can be syllabic.

[syl]	+	vowels
	−	glides, consonants

1.2.1.1.2 **Consonantal [cns].** Consonantal [cns] sounds are produced with a significant obstruction in the oral cavity. In effect, the degree of obstruction of a sound can be viewed as a spectrum progressing from the lowest, most open, vowel [a] to the stops [p, t, k]; and it would be possible to make the division between [+ cns] and [- cns] at whichever point along this spectrum seems most useful in the total system. The specification 'consonantal' [+ cns], as used in SPE and here, refers to all consonants, both obstruents and sonorants. Glides and vowels are nonconsonantal [- cns].

[cns]	+	consonants
	-	vowels and glides

1.2.1.1.3 **Sonorant [son].** Sonorant [+ son] sounds are articulated with a vocal configuration which permits spontaneous voicing.

1.2.1.1.3.1 **Definition of spontaneous voicing.** Just prior to initiation of speech, the vowel tract assumes a position somewhat different from the position which it assumes during quiet breathing. This position is called the neutral position.

The vibration of the vocal cords in relatively unimpeded sounds occurs spontaneously, with the vocal cords in the neutral position, as a result of the fast air flow from below the glottis, through the vocal cords to the supraglottal cavities. However, in the production of nonnasal consonants, there is greater obstruction in the mouth, and the nasal cavity is closed off entirely by closure of the velum. Because of this greater obstruction, the rate of air flow through the glottis is decreased considerably. This slower air flow is not sufficient to produce spontaneous voicing. Of course, obstruents can also be voiced; however, this is accomplished, presumably, by positioning the vocal cords closer together than the neutral position. For further discussion of this point, see SPE:300-302.

The feature sonorant [son] classifies the sounds of Spanish as follows. (1) Vowels are produced without sufficient obstruction to prevent spontaneous voicing, and hence are marked [+ son]. (2) Glides, although they are produced with the vocal tract somewhat more narrow than that of vowels, are not sufficiently obstructed so as to prevent spontaneous voicing. They are marked [+ son] as well. (3) Nasals, laterals, and vibrants are produced with considerable obstruction at the primary point of articulation. However, in each case, there is an alternate escape route for the air; and although the air stream is stopped in the mouth, the overall obstruction is not sufficient to suppress spontaneous voicing. These consonants are therefore marked as sonorant [+ son] as well as the vowels and glides. (4) The remaining consonants (stops, fricatives, affricates, and sibilants) do have sufficient obstruction to suppress spontaneous voicing, and are marked nonsonorant [- son]. These consonants are called 'obstruents'.

[son]	+	vowels, glides, nasals, laterals, vibrants
	−	stops, fricatives, affricates, sibilants

1.2.1.2 Application of the major class features to Spanish. Application of the major class features syllabic [syl], consonantal [cns], and sonorant [son] to Spanish establishes four major classes as illustrated in Figure 1.7.

Figure 1.7.　Feature composition of the four major classes of Spanish sounds.

	[syl]	[cns]	[son]
vowels	+	−	+
glides	−	−	+
sonorant consonants	−	+	+
obstruents	−	+	−

In many generative studies, capital letters are used in rule formulations as abbreviations for some or all of the major classes. In the chapters which follow, the following abbreviations are used:

V = vowels (all segments which are [+ syl]).
C = consonants (all segments which are [+ cns]).

Having grouped the sounds of Spanish into major classes, additional features must now be presented to differentiate each sound from all the other sounds in the same major class.

1.2.2 The classification of vowels. The difference between the various vowels is usually attributed to the various positions in which the body of the tongue may be held during articulation. The tongue may be raised or lowered, and it may be thrust forward or retracted. In addition, the lips may be rounded or left unrounded. Thus, the features required to specify the vowels phonetically are those which determine tongue position and lip rounding.

1.2.2.1 The neutral position. As explained in Section 1.2.1.1.3, it is sometimes convenient to describe the positioning of speech organs involved in the production of a given sound in terms of departure of each organ from a position which is called the 'neutral position'. The neutral position is defined as the position assumed by the entire vocal tract immediately prior to speaking. It has been determined that the neutral position for English is that of the [e] in bed. However, it is not certain that the neutral position is the same for all languages. I will assume tentatively that the neutral position for Spanish is that of the [e] of dedo 'finger'.

1.2.2.2 Features which define departures from the neutral position. The following features define departures from the neutral position which are characteristic of Spanish vowels.

1.2.2.2.1 High [high]. In the articulation of high [+ high] vowel sounds, the body of the tongue is raised considerably.

[high]	+	i, u
	−	a, e, o

1.2.2.2.2 Low [low]. In the articulation of low [+ low] vowel sounds, the body of the tongue is lowered considerably.

[low]	+	a
	−	o, e, u, i

Thus, the two height features, [high] and [low], establish three heights, as shown in Figure 1.8.

Figure 1.8. Vowel heights of Spanish characterized by the features [high] and [low].

high	[+ high]	tongue is raised considerably	i,u
mid	$\begin{bmatrix} -\text{ high} \\ -\text{ low} \end{bmatrix}$	tongue is neither raised nor lowered very much	e,o
low	[+ low]	tongue is lowered	a

Since the tongue cannot be simultaneously raised and lowered, no sound is [+ high, + low].

1.2.2.2.3 Back [back]. In the articulation of back [+ back] sounds, the body of the tongue is held in a position behind that of [ę].

[back]	+	a, o, u
	–	e, i

1.2.2.2.4 Round [rnd]. In the articulation of round [+ rnd] sounds, the lips are rounded.

[rnd]	+	o,u
	–	a,e,i

The four features [high], [low], [back], and [rnd], establish a complete classification of the five principal Spanish vowels as shown in Figure 1.9.

Figure 1.9.   Feature classification of the five principal vowels of Spanish.

	i	e	a	o	u
[high]	+	–	–	–	+
[low]	–	–	+	–	–
[back]	–	–	+	+	+
[rnd]	–	–	–	+	+

1.2.2.3 Vowel variants. Spanish vowels undergo a number of changes in quality due to the various environments in which they appear. (1) Mid and high vowels are lowered somewhat in most closed syllables (i.e. in a syllable which ends in a consonant)[2] and in contact with certain sounds (see Navarro Tomás 1968:46, 52, 59, 61 for a fuller discussion). Examples of this lowering are: tengo 'I have' [tęngo]; pongo 'I put' [pǫngo]. (2) The position of the tongue in the articulation of /a/ moves forward slightly when the /a/ is in contact with a palatal consonant, e.g. mayo 'May' [mąyo]. Similarly, the position of the tongue moves back slightly when the /a/ is in contact with /l/ or a velar consonant, e.g. malo 'bad' [mąlo]. (3) All vowels are shortened and relaxed somewhat and pronounced with less precision in certain environments, particularly, when unstressed, in a closed syllable, and in close proximity to a stressed vowel, e.g. <u>música</u> 'music' [músɪ̣ka].

Thus, in addition to the five principal vowel symbols, the following symbols are used.

[ạ]	velarized a
[ɐ]	relaxed a
[a̡]	palatalized a
[e̞]	lowered e
[ə]	relaxed e
[i̞]	lowered i
[ɪ̣]	relaxed i
[o̞]	lowered o
[ɔ̆]	relaxed o
[u̞]	lowered u
[ʊ̈]	relaxed u

These three modifications of the vowels are discussed in Sections 1.2.2.3.1 to 1.2.2.3.3.

1.2.2.3.1 Lowered mid and high vowels. The main problem in the representation of these variants is whether to use numerical values assigned by detail rules, or to rearrange the feature system so that they could all be differentiated by using only plus and minus values.

As pointed out in Section 1.1.3, numerical specifications of features are permitted at the narrow phonetic level in order to facilitate the detailed description of minute differences which exist between similar sounds. However, these numerical specifications must be introduced quite late in the derivation, in order to make possible the mechanical calculations required by the simplicity metric. Since the simplicity metric is best defined in terms of the number of feature specifications used in an analysis, it would be difficult, if not impossible, to make the necessary comparisons between alternative analyses, if 'plus' versus 'minus' specifications and numerical specifications were mixed together throughout phonological grammars.

Therefore, in reaching a decision as to whether to describe a particular difference by plus versus minus specifications or by numerical specifications, it is necessary to consider the possible phonemic status of that difference in the languages of the world. In this connection, it is clear that the phonetic difference between regular and lowered mid vowels ([e] versus [e̞] and [o] versus [o̞]) is large enough so that it may be phonemic in some languages. If this is so, it is possible to classify a seven-vowel system by using only plus and minus specifications for the features which have been defined thus far (see Figure 1.10). However, considerable revision of this system would be required to account for [i̯] and [u̯] if only plus and minus specifications were used.

Figure 1.10. Classification of a seven-vowel system by 'plus' and 'minus' values of four features.

	i	e	ę	a	ǫ	o	u
[high]	+	−	−	−	−	−	+
[low]	−	−	+	+	+	−	−
[back]	−	−	−	+	+	+	+
[rnd]	−	−	−	−	+	+	+

Since the phonetic differences between [i] and [i̯] and between [u] and [u̯] are very slight, it is unlikely that either pair of sounds occurs in phonemic contrast in any language.[3] Therefore, the lowering of Spanish high vowels, at least, can be described by a Detail Rule. Moreover, the high and mid vowels are all lowered in roughly the same environment, and therefore the lowering of all four vowels /i/, /u/, /e/, and /o/ must be described by a single rule. For this reason, it seems that a conversion from plus and minus to numerical values of the feature [high] is the correct way to account fully for this lowering phenomenon.

Detail Rules (1.4) through (1.7) convert the five vowels specified at the broad phonetic level in Figure 1.11 to the nine vowels specified at the narrow phonetic level in Figure 1.12.

Figure 1.11. Five principal vowels of Spanish specified at the broad phonetic level.

	i	e	a	o	u
[high]	+	−	−	−	+
[low]	−	−	+	−	−
[back]	−	−	+	+	+
[rnd]	−	−	−	+	+

(1.4) [+ high] ---> [5 high]

(1.5) [+ low] ---> [∅ high]

(1.6) $\begin{bmatrix} - \text{ high} \\ - \text{ low} \end{bmatrix}$ ---➤ [3 high]

(1.7) $\begin{bmatrix} \text{n high} \\ - \text{ low} \end{bmatrix}$ ---➤ [n-1 high] / ___C -

Figure 1.12.　Nine Spanish vowels specified at the narrow phonetic level.

	i	i̯	e	ẹ	a	ǫ	o	u̯	u
[high]	5	4	3	2	Ø	2	3	4	5
[low]	-	-	-	-	+	-	-	-	-
[back]	-	-	-	-	+	+	+	+	+
[rnd]	-	-	-	-	-	+	+	+	+

Rule (1.7) is the lowering rule for mid and high vowels and states that a vowel which is minus low (i.e. any vowel other than [a]) is lowered by one level before a syllable final consonant (C -). The hyphen (-) represents a syllable boundary. This is somewhat of an oversimplification. The exact environment for this rule varies slightly from vowel to vowel. (See Navarro Tomás 1968: 46, 52, 59, 61).

1.2.2.3.2 Palatalized and velarized low vowels. In his description of palatalized and velarized low vowels, Navarro Tomás does not provide an additional symbol for palatalized a. It seems to me that something not entirely unlike the Detail Rules procedure used in Section 1.2.2.3.1 must be implied in Navarro's practice of pointing out a distinction but failing to represent it at the phonetic level. Furthermore, since the distinction is not, to my knowledge, phonemic in any language,[4] a representation using numerical values specified by a Detail Rule seems most reasonable. Moreover, a more generalized version of the Detail Rule used to palatalize and velarize /a/ can be used to assign numerical values of backness to the high and mid vowels as well, and thus provide a feature analog of the vowel triangle. Assuming that [a̧] and [a] are raised one level as they become palatalized and velarized, the Spanish vowel phones can be displayed in a vowel triangle as shown in Figure 1.13.

Detail Rules (1.4) through (1.9) yield the feature values shown in Figure 1.13. Rule (1.8) palatalizes (i.e. raises and fronts) /a/ in contact with certain consonants; and it velarizes /a/ in contact with certain other consonants. (For a full specification of these environments, see Navarro Tomás 1968: 55-57.) Detail Rule (1.9) which assigns the numerical values to the feature [back] makes use of the 'alpha' notation. Alpha

Figure 1.13.   Triangle display of Spanish vowels.

[high]	5	i									u
	4		i̯						ʮ		
	3			e				o			
	2				e̯			ǫ			
	1					a̯		a̦			
	Ø						a				

[back]	1	2	3	4	5	6	7	8	9	10	11

(α) is a variable which can be either plus or minus. Its value must remain the same wherever it appears for any given application of the rule. Therefore, if the segment in question is [+ back], the value of alpha is plus, and the numerical value of the feature [back] is [(6 + n) back] where n is that segment's value for [high]. For example, [o], which is [3 high] is [(6 + 3) back], or [9 back].

A comparison of Figures 1.13 and 1.14 shows that each segment has values of the features [high] and [back] which assign it to the appropriate position on the vowel triangle.

Figure 1.14.   Numerical feature classification of 11 Spanish vowel phones at the narrow phonetic level.

	i	i̯	e	e̯	a̯	a	a̦	ǫ	o	ʮ	u
[high]	5	4	3	2	1	0	1	2	3	4	5
[low]	-	-	-	-	+	+	+	-	-	-	-
[back]	1	2	3	4	5	6	7	8	9	10	11
[rnd]	-	-	-	-	-	-	-	+	+	+	+

(1.4)   [+ high] $\longrightarrow$ [5 high]

(1.5)   [+ low] $\longrightarrow$ [Ø high]

(1.6) $\begin{bmatrix} - \text{ high} \\ - \text{ low} \end{bmatrix}$ $\longrightarrow$ [3 high]

(1.7) $\begin{bmatrix} n \text{ high} \\ - \text{ low} \end{bmatrix}$ $\longrightarrow$ [n-1 high] / ___C-

(1.8)   [+ low] $\longrightarrow$ $\begin{cases} \begin{bmatrix} 1 \text{ high} \\ - \text{ back} \end{bmatrix} & / \text{ ___x} \\ [1 \text{ high}] & / \text{ ___y} \end{cases}$

(1.9)   V $\longrightarrow$ [6 α n back] / $\begin{bmatrix} \overline{n \text{ high}} \\ α \text{ back} \end{bmatrix}$

1.2.2.3.3 Relaxed vowels. The Spanish vowel phones described in the previous sections are all produced with more

precision and muscular tension than are English vowels. In
feature terminology, they are [+ tense]. The feature
[tense] is defined as follows: Tense sounds are produced with
considerable precision and muscular tension. Lax (nontense)
sounds are articulated somewhat less precisely and with less
tension. This feature is discussed in greater detail in Section
1.2.4.2.1.3. The relaxed vowels which occur frequently in a
syllable next to a stressed syllable differ from the vowels which
have been discussed thus far in that they are nontense
[- tense]. Although there are 11 distinct tense vowel phones,
the finer differences represented by the symbols in Figure 1.14
are neutralized when a vowel is relaxed [- tense]. Therefore,
there are only five lax vowels, one corresponding to each vowel
phoneme.

1.2.3 The classification of glides. Glides can be subclassified in two ways, (1) on-glides versus off-glides (Section
1.2.3.1 and (2) high versus nonhigh glides (Section 1.2.3.2).

1.2.3.1 On-glides versus off-glides. Navarro Tomás posits
four glides: two semiconsonants (on-glides), [j] and [w] which
occur before another vowel, e.g. [bjen] bien 'well' and [bwen]
buen 'good' and two semivowels (off-glides) [i̯] and [u̯] which
occur after another vowel, e.g. [bei̯nte] veinte 'twenty' and
[deu̯da] deuda 'debt'.
Navarro (1968:49) describes the difference between semiconsonants and semivowels as follows:

...[j] differs from [i̯] in that it is articulated with a completely different movement of the vocal organs: In the
articulation of [i̯], the vocal tract changes from a relatively open position to a more closed position, whereas in
the articulation of [j], the vocal tract changes from a
relatively closed position to a more open position.

However, when we consider that the environment of a semiconsonant is ___ V while that of a semivowel is V ___ , it seems
natural that an opening gesture would result before a vowel
and a closing gesture would follow one. Thus it seems that
any difference between the semiconsonant and the semivowel
can be attributed to the effect of 'going from one sound to another'; and the assumption can be made that, in terms of the
perceptual reality described in systematic phonetics, the sounds
are identical.
Note that the environments of on-glides and off-glides do not
represent a typical case of allophonic conditioning or complemen-
tary distribution. The difference between on-glides and off-
glides is an automatic universal result of the contact with other
sounds. However, the typical case of allophonic conditioning is
not universal. For example, in Spanish, lax obstruents are
pronounced as stops initially and as fricatives medially (the

environments are slightly more complex, see Section 3.2).
But this fricative articulation is not an automatic consequence
of the medial position, nor is it universal. Furthermore,
there are languages which lack this alternation (e.g. English);
and it would not be unexpected if a language had these two
allophones with the opposite distribution (i.e. fricatives
initially and stops medially).

However, it is inconceivable that a language might have sequences such as C SV V or V SC C. Furthermore, there are
other types of automatic conditioning phenomena which are not
traditionally accounted for by establishing multiple allophones.
For example, it can be shown instrumentally that the beginning
contour of a vowel (e.g. [a]) is quite different when preceded
by, for example, [p], from the beginning of that same vowel
when preceded by [k].

I take the position, therefore, that the systematic phonemic
distinction is between a syllabic nucleus [+ syl] (a vowel) and
a sound that is nonnuclear [- syl] (a glide), and I represent
all high glides, whether they appear before or after the syllabic nucleus, simply as [j] and [w].

1.2.3.2 Nonhigh glides. In his discussion of sequences of
nonhigh vowels, Navarro (1968:67) describes a modification
suffered by [e] and [o] in contact with another vowel as
follows: 'They are closed somewhat, shortened, and relaxed,
and articulated with a slightly more open version of the articulatory gesture which produces the glides [j] and [w].' Examples are poeta 'poet' [pǫeta] and teatro 'theatre' [tǫatro]. In
spite of his own analogy with the high glides, Navarro chooses
to represent these sounds by the same symbols that he uses
for relaxed e and o. He gives as his reason 'the desire not
to overcomplicate the transcription'. However, a close examination reveals that there is an important difference between the
relaxed mid vowels and the mid glides: the relaxed mid vowels
must be [+ syllabic] because they occur in syllables having no
other possible nuclei, e.g. the e in lunes 'Monday', and
hermanos 'brothers', etc. On the other hand, the mid glides
always occur next to another vowel and therefore might be
[- syllabic], e.g. the e in teatro 'theatre'. Since Navarro's
own description strongly suggests that this is so, I will assume
(as does Harris 1970) that this is the case. Furthermore,
Harris provides evidence to the effect that the low vowel [a]
shows analogical low glides. Therefore, I assume that Spanish
has potentially five glides, one corresponding to each of the
five major vowels.[5] These five glides can be fully classified
by applying to them the features in Section 1.2.2.2 to classify
the vowels.

Thus the features introduced so far are able adequately to
classify (as shown in Figure 1.15) all those broad phonetic
segments which are [- consonantal].

[+ syllabic]	[-syllabic]
i	j
u	w
e	e̥
o	o̥
a	ḁ

Figure 1.15. Feature classification of all nonconsonantal segments at the broad phonetic level.

	i	e	a	o	u	ɪ	ə	ɐ	c̣	ü	j	e̬	ɐ̬	ɔ̬	w
[syl]	+	+	+	+	+	+	+	+	+	+	-	-	-	-	-
[high]	+	-	-	-	+	+	-	-	-	+	+	-	-	-	+
[low]	-	-	+	-	-	-	-	+	-	-	-	-	+	-	-
[back]	-	-	+	+	+	-	-	+	+	+	-	-	+	+	+
[rnd]	-	-	-	+	+	-	-	-	+	+	-	-	-	+	+
[tns]	+	+	+	+	+	-	-	-	-	-	+	+	+	+	+

1.2.4 The classification of obstruents. In the classification of obstruents, features are used to specify: (1) point of articulation (Section 1.2.4.1) and (2) manner of articulation (Section 1.2.4.2).

1.2.4.1 Point of articulation. Since some of the features discussed in connection with vowels also figure in the point of articulation of consonants, these features will be discussed first.

1.2.4.1.1 The vowel features as applied to consonants. As defined in Section 1.2.2.2.1, the feature specification [+ high] indicates that the body of the tongue is raised in the production of the sound. The body of the tongue is raised in the production of palatal and velar consonants, but not in the production of other consonants.

[high]	+	velars, palatals (i.e. k, g, x, ĉ, l, y)
	-	all others (e.g. b, d, f, s, etc.)

As defined in Section 1.2.2.2.3, the feature specification [+ back] indicates that the body of the tongue is retracted in the production of the sound. The body of the tongue is

retracted in the production of velar consonants, but not in the
production of other Spanish consonants.

[back]	+	velars
	-	all others

As defined in Section 1.2.2.2.4, the feature specification
[+ rnd] indicates that the lips are rounded in the production
of the sound.

In his discussion of the semivowel [w], Navarro Tomás (1968:
64) states that when it "occurs between vowels ahuecar ([awekar]
'to hollow out', WWC) or in absolute initial position hueso
([weso] 'bone', WWC), the onset of its articulation takes on
even more the characteristics of a consonant...similar to a
labialized [ǥ]". The difference between this fricative and the
sound [ǥ] can best be characterized by marking [ǥ^W] [+ round]
and [ǥ] [- round]. All other Spanish consonants are [- round].

[rnd]	+	labialized velar fricative [ǥ^W]
	-	all others

In addition, some languages have consonants which are [+ low]
(the body of the tongue is lowered from the neutral position in
the articulation of the sound); however, in Spanish, all consonants are [- low].

1.2.4.1.2 Additional features for point of articulation. The
main additional features required to establish the basic points
of articulation are (1) an arbitrary subdivision of the oral
cavity into front and back parts ([anterior] (Section
1.2.4.1.2.1)), and (2) a feature which specifies whether the
blade of the tongue is raised from the neutral position
([coronal]). (The blade of the tongue is the front part, including both the tip and the flat part immediately behind the
tip.) (Section 1.2.4.1.2.2.)

1.2.4.1.2.1 Anterior [ant]. 'Anterior sounds are produced
with an obstruction that is located in front of the palato-
alveolar region of the mouth; nonanterior sounds are produced
without such an obstruction' (SPE:304).

[ant]	+	bilabials, labio-dentals, dentals, alveolars
	-	palato-alveolars, palatals, velars

1.2.4.1.2.2 **Coronal [cor].** In the articulation of [+ cor] sounds, the blade of the tongue is raised from the neutral position.

[cor]	+	palato-alveolars, alveolars, dentals, interdentals
	-	velars, palatals, labio-dentals, bilabials

The four features [high], [back], [ant], and [cor] can be used to subdivide the points of articulation into six groups similar to what Alarcos (1968:71ff.) calls 'orders' as illustrated in Figure 1.16.

Figure 1.16. Points of articulation grouped into orders.

	labials, labio-dentals	inter-dentals, dentals, alveolars	palato-alveolars	retroflex (e.g.: Cast. s)	palatals	velars
[high]	-	-	+	-	+	+
[back]	-	-	-	-	-	+
[ant]	+	+	-	-	-	-
[cor]	-	+	+	+	-	-

1.2.4.1.2.3 **Dental [den].** In the articulation of dental [+ den] sounds, the teeth are used as one of the primary articulators.

[den]	+	labio-dentals, interdentals, dentals
	-	all others

Thus this feature distinguishes labio-dentals [+ den] from bilabials [- den], and dentals [+ den] from alveolars [- den]. These distinctions are drawn at the systematic phonetic level, although it is not necessary from the standpoint of Spanish phonology to subclassify the orders of points of articulation

shown in Figure 1.16. The various sounds which occur in each
order either do not contrast with each other phonemically
(e.g. bilabial [m] and labio-dental [m̥]), or can be differentiated using a manner of articulation feature (for example, bilabial [p] [+ occlusive] and labio-dental [f] [- occlusive]).

In previous studies (e.g. SPE and Harris 1969), the distinctions described here by the feature [dental] have been characterized by another feature, namely [distributed]. This feature
is defined as follows: Distributed [+ dis] sounds are produced
with a construction that extends for a considerable distance
along the direction of the air flow; nondistributed [- dis]
sounds are produced with a constriction that extends only for
a short distance in this direction.

[dis]	+	bilabials, alveolars
	-	labio-dentals, dentals

It seems likely that articulations which involve the cutting
edge of either the upper or lower teeth involve shorter con-
strictions than articulations involving, for example, both lips.
Therefore, the use of the feature [distributed] in SPE and in
Harris (1969) to distinguish bilabials [+ dis] from labio-dentals
[- dis] seems correct. However, it is not clear that the dental
sounds [t] and [d], which involve the tip of the tongue and
the back surface of the upper teeth have a shorter construction
than do alveolars. Examination of anatomical drawings for these
sounds as compared to [n] suggests that the dentals, in fact,
have a longer constriction than the alveolars (see Figure 1.17
and Navarro Tomás 1968:96, 111).[6] Therefore, Harris' use of
the feature [distributed] to distinguish alveolars [+ dis] from
dentals [- dis] seems questionable.

Figure 1.17.   Sketches of the articulations for alveolar [n]
and dental [t] and [d].

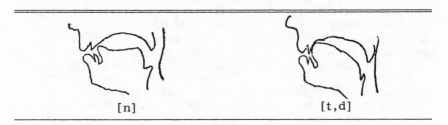

[n]   [t,d]

Because of this doubt, I have made the distinctions mentioned
earlier in this section using the feature [dental] rather than
[distributed]. There are other distinctions effected by the

feature [distributed] which cannot be accomplished by the feature [dental]. For example, Harris (1969:192) uses the feature
[distributed] to distinguish American [x] [+ dis] from Castilian
[X] [- dis]. However, Harris' drawings (see Figure 1.18) suggest that the construction of the latter sound is also lower than
that of the former, and therefore, the two sounds could be distinguished by the feature [high] (either by marking [x] [+ high]
and [X] [- high], or by assigning different numeric values for
the feature [high] to the two sounds at the narrow phonetic
level).

Figure 1.18. Anatomical sketches of the articulation for
American [x] and Castilian [X].

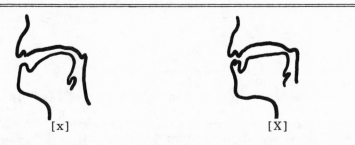

[x]   [X]

1.2.4.1.3 **Dental versus interdental sounds.** In Spanish,
there are dental sounds which are articulated with the tip of
the tongue and the inner surface of the upper teeth: [t],
[d], and [đ]. There are also interdental sounds which are
articulated using the tip of the tongue and the cutting edge of
the upper teeth: [θ] and its voiced variant [z̧] (e.g.
[xuz̧ɣar] juzgar 'to judge'). As pointed out by Navarro (1968:
100), there is a difference between the fricative [đ] and the
voiced variant of /θ/: [z̧]. According to Navarro, [đ] is 'less
interdental, more relaxed, softer, and shorter than [z̧]'.
The notation 'less interdental' suggests that a continuum of
numerical feature specifications is the correct way to express
the exact location of the tip of the tongue in the articulation
of these sounds. Furthermore, as indicated by Navarro, the
point of articulation is by no means the only phonetic difference between these two sounds, nor even the most important
one. The other attributes of [đ] as compared to [z̧] all suggest that the most important feature which differentiates the
two segments is the feature [tense]. [đ] is lax, whereas [z̧]
is tense. Therefore it is not necessary to distinguish between
these two segments by reference to the dental vs. interdental
contrast. Furthermore, it seems unlikely that any language has
two segments in phonemic contrast which differ only in that one
of them is dental and the other is interdental. Therefore, I
have subsumed interdentals and dentals under one category

(which I call 'dental') and have not represented this distinction in my feature system.

At the narrow phonetic level, the distinction could be made explicit by means of Detail Rules (such as Rules (1.10) and (1.11)) specifying the exact degree of anteriority in numerical values.

(1.10)   [+ dental, - occlusive, + tense] ([θ]) --→ [5 ant]
(1.11)   [+ dental] (all others)   --→ [4 ant]

1.2.4.1.4 The points of articulation as classified by the features. The features discussed in the preceding sections classify the points of articulation as shown in Figure 1.19.

Figure 1.19.   Distinctive feature classification of the points of articulation in Spanish.

	bilabial	labio-dental	dental	alveolar	retro-flex	palato-alveolar	palatal	velar
[high]	-	-	-	-	-	+	+	+
[back]	-	-	-	-	-	-	-	+
[ant]	+	+	+	+	-	-	-	-
[cor]	-	-	+	+	+	+	-	-
[den]	-	+	+	-	-	-	-	-

1.2.4.2 Manner of articulation. Among the obstruents, there are the following manners of articulation in Spanish: stops, fricatives, affricates, and sibilants (see Figure 1.20).

Figure 1.20.   Manners of articulation in Spanish.

	voiceless	voiced
stops	p,t,k	b,d,g
fricatives	f,θ,x	ƀ,đ,y,ǥ,ǥ^w
affricates	ĉ	ŷ
sibilants	s	z

1.2.4.2.1 Features which define manner of articulation. In the generative framework, these manners of articulation are classified by the features described in the sections which follow.

1.2.4.2.1.1 Occlusive [ocl]. In the articulation of occlusive [+ ocl] sounds, the air flow in the speech tract is blocked by an occlusion at the primary point of articulation.

[ocl]	+	stops, affricates
	−	fricatives, sibilants

This feature replaces the feature [continuant] as defined in Jakobson, Fant, and Halle (1963).[7] In the classification of obstruents, the new feature is simply the converse of the older one (i.e. [+ occlusive] equals [− continuant] and vice versa). However, as explained in Section 1.2.5.2.3, the new feature classifies the sonorant consonants in a way which is different from the classification effected by the old feature. Any sound which has complete blockage at the primary point of articulation is [+ occlusive] even though in the case of some sounds (e.g. nasals and laterals) the air escapes via an alternate route and the sound is [+ continuant] according to the Jakobson, Fant, and Halle definition.

1.2.4.2.1.2 Instantaneous release [ins]. The feature instantaneous release [ins] applies only to sounds with complete blockage of the airstream and subclassifies those sounds with respect to the type of release. Sounds which are marked [+ ins] are characterized by an instantaneous or very rapid release of the occlusion. Those marked [− ins] have a gradual release of the occlusion. This feature therefore distinguishes between stops [+ ins] and affricates [− ins]. All segments which are [− ocl] are automatically [− ins], as are nasals and laterals.

[ins]	+	stops
	−	affricates, all other sounds

1.2.4.2.1.3 Tense [tns]. Tense [+ tns] sounds are produced with considerable precision and muscular tension. Lax (nontense) [− tns] sounds are articulated somewhat less precisely and with less tension.

[tns]	+	p,t,k,s,θ,f,x,ĉ
	−	b,d,g,ƀ,đ,ǥ,y,ŷ

For most Spanish sounds, the feature [tns] is simply the converse of the traditional term 'voiced'. However, this corre-
spondence is not universal. It does not even apply to all
Spanish sounds; [r̃], which is voiced, is [+ ten]. In addition, Harris (1969:40ff.) in his treatment of certain assimilation phenomena, marks sounds such as [z] as [+ ten, + voi].
(That is, when /s/ assimilates to the following consonant, as
for example in the word mismo 'same' [mizmo], it takes on the
voicing of the /m/, but it retains its own value for the feature
[tense], that is [+ tns]. Therefore, two separate features are
needed, one to specify tensity and another to specify voicing.

1.2.4.2.1.4 Voiced [+ voi]. There is a problem associated
with the definition of the feature [voiced] because it is not
entirely accurate to divide sounds simply into two groups
(voiced and voiceless). Measurements and other phonetic in-
vestigations discussed in Lisker and Abramson (1964), Kim
(1965), SPE, and Harris (1969), indicate that it is more accurate to classify some sounds, for example, stops, according to
the relative time of onset of vocal cord vibration when a stop
is followed by a vowel. Lisker and Abramson (1964) distinguish four possible onset times: (1) vibration starts before
the release of the occlusion (e.g. Spanish voiced stops), (2)
vibration starts at approximately the same time as the release
of the occlusion (e.g. Spanish voiceless stops), (3) vibration
starts just after the release of the occlusion, and (4) vibration starts considerably after the release of the occlusion (e.g.
English initial [p, t, k]).
Chomsky and Halle have taken the position that these four
onset times are the result of the interaction of four features--
[tense], [voiced] (vocal cords not held too widely apart to
vibrate), [glottal constriction] (the glottal aperture is narrowed
beyond its neutral position), and [heightened subglottal pres-
sure] (the pressure below the glottis is increased).
Harris (1969), working within this framework and based upon
comparisons of Spanish and Korean voiceless stops, has concluded that Spanish [p, t, k] (in the production of which the
onset of voicing substantially coincides with stop release)
should be marked [+ voiced, + glottal constriction, + heightened
subglottal pressure]. That is, Harris assumes that, although
these stops are produced with the vocal cords held in the voicing position, they are not 'voiced through' because the vibration is suppressed by the two other factors [glottal constriction]
and [heightened subglottal pressure].
However, in a second article, Lisker and Abramson (1971)
have reasserted their position that onset of voicing is being
directly controlled by the speaker rather than indirectly by
means of the Chomsky and Halle feature configuration. Their
conclusion, if correct, poses a problem for the theory of binary
features. It would seem that the most logical feature

representation of Lisker and Abramson's hypothesis would be a
four-valued feature of voicing defined as follows:

[1 voice]:   onset of voicing precedes stop release
[2 voice]:   onset coincides
[3 voice]:   onset lags somewhat
[4 voice]:   onset lags greatly

If it were the case that no language had phonemically contrasting stops belonging to more than two of the foregoing
categories, then it would be possible to use [+ voiced] for all
distinctions, and specify the onset times indicated by [+ voiced]
and [- voiced] with Detail Rules for each language.

Since Spanish has but two categories of stops, this is the approach that is adopted here. Thus, the traditional designations
[b, d, g] = [+ voiced] and [p, t, k] = [- voiced] are maintained. However, it must be emphasized that this procedure
in no way constitutes a solution to the theoretical problem. The
question of what other features (in addition to [+ voiced] as defined here) would be required to classify fully the obstruents
of a language having more than two onset times in phonemic
contrast, still remains unsolved.

Thus, in this study, the specification [+ voiced] means that
the vocal cords are held in such a position as to vibrate during
the production of the sound.

[voi]	+	b,d,g
	-	p,t,k

1.2.4.2.2 **A note on stridency.** Stridency is an acoustic
property which, among other things, distinguishes sibilants
from fricatives. The definition of the feature [strident] presented in SPE (p. 329) is formulated as follows: 'strident
sounds are marked acoustically by greater noisiness than their
nonstrident counterparts'. Moreover, the authors suggest the
articulatory causes of this greater noisiness ('a rougher surface,
a faster rate of flow, and an angle of incidence closer to ninety
degrees will all contribute to greater stridency'). It is possible, therefore, that this feature could be reformulated as one
or more articulatory features. However, Harris (1969:200) has
shown that it is possible to predict completely the stridency
values of all Spanish sounds (and of many others) in terms of
other features, and he therefore questions the existence of
[strident] as a feature. Because it is essentially an acoustic
feature, and because it is not needed for the classification of

Spanish sounds, the feature [strident] is omitted from the inventory used in this presentation.

The features discussed in Sections 1.2.4.1 through 1.2.4.2.1.4 can be used to classify the principal obstruents of Spanish, as shown in Figure 1.21.[8]

Figure 1.21. Distinctive feature classification of the principal obstruents of Spanish.

	p	t	ĉ	k	b	d	ŷ	g	ƀ	đ	y	ǥ	ǥʷ	f	θ	s	x
[high]	−	−	+	+	−	−	+	+	−	−	+	+	+	−	−	−	+
[back]	−	−	−	+	−	−	−	+	−	−	−	+	+	−	−	−	+
[ant]	+	+	−	−	+	+	−	−	+	+	−	−	−	+	+	−	−
[cor]	−	+	+	−	−	+	−	−	−	+	−	−	−	−	+	+	−
[den]	−	+	−	−	−	+	−	−	−	+	−	−	−	+	+	−	−
[ocl]	+	+	+	+	+	+	+	+	−	−	−	−	−	−	−	−	−
[ins]	+	+	−	+	+	+	−	+	−	−	−	−	−	−	−	−	−
[tns]	+	+	+	+	−	−	−	−	−	−	−	−	−	+	+	+	+
[voi]	−	−	−	−	+	+	+	+·	+	+	+	+	+	−	−	−	−
[rnd]	−	−	−	−	−	−	−	−	−	−	−	−	+	−	−	−	−

1.2.5 The classification of sonorant consonants. Many of the same point of articulation features used for obstruents are used for the classification of sonorants as well. In addition, two other manner features are needed.

1.2.5.1 Additional features which define manner of articulation among sonorant consonants. There are additional features which define the manner of articulation among the sonorant consonants, namely, (1) nasal [nas] (Section 1.2.5.1.1) and (2) lateral [lat] (Section 1.2.5.1.2).

1.2.5.1.1 Nasal [nas]. In the articulation of nasal [+ nas] sounds, the velum is lowered allowing air to escape through the nose.

[nas]	+	m,m̰,ņ,n,ǹ,ñ, ŋ
	−	all other consonants

1.2.5.1.2 **Lateral [lat].** In the articulation of lateral [+ lat] sounds, the sides of the tongue are lowered, allowing air to escape along the sides of the mouth.

[lat]	+	ḷ,l,ĺ,ĩ
	-	all other sounds

Figure 1.22 represents the application of the features presented thus far to the sonorant consonants (i.e. to all segments marked [- syl, + cns, + son]).

Figure 1.22. Distinctive feature classification of the sonorant consonants of Spanish.

	m	m̭	n̩	n	ǹ	ñ	ŋ	ḷ	l	ì	ĩ	r	r̃
[nas]	+	+	+	+	+	+	+	-	-	-	-	-	-
[lat]	-	-	-	-	-	-	-	+	+	+	+	-	-
[high]	-	-	-	-	+	+	+	-	-	+	+	-	-
[back]	-	-	-	-	-	-	+	-	-	-	-	-	-
[ant]	+	+	+	+	-	-	-	+	+	-	-	+	+
[cor]	-	-	+	+	+	-	-	+	+	+	-	+	+
[den]	-	+	+	-	-	-	-	+	-	-	-	-	-
[ocl]	+	+	+	+	+	+	+	+	+	+	+	-	-
[ins]	-	-	-	-	-	-	-	-	-	-	-	-	-
[tns]	-	-	-	-	-	-	-	-	-	-	-	-	+
[voi]	+	+	+	+	+	+	+	+	+	+	+	+	+

1.2.5.2 **Application of previously defined features to the sonorant consonants.** The application of previously defined features to the sonorant consonants includes (1) the elimination of interdentals (Section 1.5.2.1), (2) a discussion of palato-alveolar vs. palatal consonants (Section 1.2.5.2.2), and (3) a discussion of the feature [occlusive] as applied to sonorant consonants (Section 1.2.5.2.3).

1.2.5.2.1 **Elimination of interdentals.** For reasons discussed in Section 1.2.5.3, the distinction between dentals and interdentals is not maintained in this study at the broad phonetic level. Thus, the symbols [n̪] and [l̪] have been eliminated, and the symbols [n̩] and [ḷ] include sounds with the interdental articulation. As explained earlier, the exact location of the articulation can be made precise by Detail Rules.

1.2.5.2.2 Palato-alveolar versus palatal. In most treatments of Spanish nasals, the distinction between palatal [ñ] and palato-alveolar [ǹ] is not drawn. The distinction is discussed, however, in Quilis and Fernández (1969), and a distinctive feature analysis of it is presented in Harris (1969). The extension of this distinction to the laterals ([l] versus [ḽ]) was suggested to me by Eliot Woodaman (personal communication).

1.2.5.2.3 The feature [occlusive] as applied to sonorant consonants. As noted earlier, in the production of nasals and laterals there is complete blockage at the primary point of articulation; however, air is allowed to escape via another route--in the case of nasals, through the nose, and in the case of laterals, via the sides of the mouth. Therefore, nasals and laterals are [+ occlusive] according to the definition given in Section 1.2.4.2.1.1.

There may also be some doubt concerning the classification of Spanish [r] and [r̃]. As explained in SPE, the contact between the tongue and the alveolar ridge in taps and trills is not effected directly by placing the tongue in contact with the palate, as it is in the articulation of nasals, laterals, and [+ occlusive] obstruents. Rather, the movement of the tongue upwards to make contact is caused 'by the drop in pressure which occurs inside the passage between the tip of the tongue and the palate when the air flows rapidly through it (Bernoulli effect)' (SPE:318). The definition of the feature [occlusive] is to be interpreted as excluding such momentary contact which, as Chomsky and Halle put it, is 'a secondary effect of narrowing the cavity'.

One may legitimately question the wisdom of substituting the new feature [occlusive] for the older feature [continuant] (as defined in Jakobson, Fant, and Halle 1963), since the older feature is closer to the traditional term 'stop'. In theory, either feature, or even both, might be included in the universal set of features. There is no a priori basis for choice. However, substantial evidence in favor of the newer feature used in this study is given in Sections 3.1.2.1 and 3.2.4.

1.3 Matrix of sounds of Spanish as classified by features at the broad phonetic level. Figure 1.23 presents a complete classification of the sounds of Spanish at the broad phonetic level. In the chapters which follow, the systematic use and the organization of these sounds are discussed.

NOTES

1. I have established and defined these two levels as a matter of convenience. However, one question which must be answered by linguists is: What levels of representation of utterances are linguistically significant? I am not making the claim that each of these levels is of theoretical significance.

	i	e	a	o	u	į	ę	ą	ǫ	c̣	c̈	j̈	ĵ	ę̃	ą̃	ǫ̃	w	r	r̃	j̃	l	l′	l̦	l̂	m	m̦	ɱ	n	ń	ñ	ŋ	p	t	c̃	k	p̈	ẗ	k̈	b	d	ÿ	g	ƀ	đ	y	ǥ	ǥʷ	ƀ̥	đ̥	ǥ̥	f	θ	s	x	f̈	θ̈	ṣ	ẍ
[cns]	–	–	–	–	–	–	–	–	–	–	–	–	–	–	–	–	–	+	+	+	+	+	+	+	+	+	+	+	+	+	+	+	+	+	+	+	+	+	+	+	+	+	+	+	+	+	+	+	+	+	+	+	+	+	+	+	+	+
[syl]	+	+	+	+	+	+	+	+	+	+	+	–	–	–	–	–	–	–	–	–	–	–	–	–	–	–	–	–	–	–	–	–	–	–	–	–	–	–	–	–	–	–	–	–	–	–	–	–	–	–	–	–	–	–	–	–	–	–
[nas]	–	–	–	–	–	+	+	+	+	–	–	–	–	+	+	+	–	–	–	–	–	–	–	–	+	+	+	+	+	+	+	–	–	–	–	–	–	–	–	–	–	–	–	–	–	–	–	–	–	–	–	–	–	–	–	–	–	–
[lat]	–	–	–	–	–	–	–	–	–	–	–	–	–	–	–	–	–	–	–	–	+	+	+	+	–	–	–	–	–	–	–	–	–	–	–	–	–	–	–	–	–	–	–	–	–	–	–	–	–	–	–	–	–	–	–	–	–	–
[son]	+	+	+	+	+	+	+	+	+	+	+	+	+	+	+	+	+	+	+	+	+	+	+	+	+	+	+	+	+	+	+	–	–	–	–	–	–	–	–	–	–	–	–	–	–	–	–	–	–	–	–	–	–	–	–	–	–	–
[ant]	–	–	+	–	–	–	–	+	–	–	–	–	–	–	+	–	–	+	+	–	+	+	+	–	+	+	+	+	–	–	–	+	+	–	–	+	+	–	+	+	–	–	+	+	–	–	–	+	+	–	+	+	+	–	+	+	+	–
[low]	–	–	+	–	–	–	–	+	–	–	–	–	–	–	+	–	–	–	–	–	–	–	–	–	–	–	–	–	–	–	–	–	–	–	–	–	–	–	–	–	–	–	–	–	–	–	–	–	–	–	–	–	–	–	–	–	–	–
[back]	–	–	–	+	+	–	–	–	+	–	+	–	–	–	–	+	+	–	–	–	–	–	–	+	–	–	–	–	–	–	+	–	–	–	+	–	–	+	–	–	–	+	–	–	–	+	+	–	–	+	–	–	–	+	–	–	–	+
[high]	+	–	–	–	+	+	–	–	–	+	+	+	+	–	–	–	+	–	–	+	–	–	–	+	–	–	–	–	+	–	+	–	–	+	+	–	–	+	–	–	+	+	–	–	+	+	+	–	–	+	–	–	–	+	–	–	–	+
[rnd]	–	–	–	+	+	–	–	–	+	–	–	–	–	–	–	+	+	–	–	–	–	–	–	–	–	–	–	–	–	–	–	–	–	–	–	–	–	–	–	–	–	–	–	–	–	–	+	–	–	–	–	–	–	–	–	–	–	–
[cor]	–	–	–	–	–	–	–	–	–	+	–	–	+	–	–	–	–	–	–	+	–	–	+	–	–	–	–	+	+	+	–	–	+	+	–	–	+	–	–	+	+	–	–	+	+	–	–	–	+	–	–	+	+	–	–	+	+	–
[tns]	+	–	–	–	+	–	–	–	+	+	+	+	+	–	–	+	+	–	–	–	–	+	–	+	–	–	–	–	–	–	+	–	–	–	+	+	+	+	–	–	–	+	–	–	–	–	–	–	–	–	–	–	–	+	+	+	+	+
[ocl]	–	–	–	–	–	–	–	–	–	–	–	–	–	–	–	–	–	–	–	+	–	–	–	+	+	+	+	+	+	+	+	+	+	+	+	+	+	+	+	+	+	+	–	–	–	–	–	–	–	–	–	–	–	–	–	–	–	–
[ins]	–	–	–	–	–	–	–	–	–	–	–	–	–	–	–	–	–	–	+	+	–	–	–	–	+	+	+	+	+	+	+	–	+	+	+	–	+	+	–	+	+	+	–	–	–	–	–	+	+	+	+	+	+	–	+	+	+	–
[den]	–	–	–	–	–	–	–	–	–	–	–	–	–	–	–	–	–	–	–	–	–	–	–	–	–	–	–	–	–	–	–	–	–	–	–	–	–	–	–	–	–	–	–	–	–	–	–	–	–	–	–	–	–	–	–	–	–	–
[voi]	+	+	+	+	+	–	–	–	–	–	–	–	–	–	–	–	+	+	+	+	+	+	+	+	+	+	+	+	+	+	+	–	–	–	–	–	–	–	+	+	+	+	+	+	+	+	+	–	–	–	–	–	–	–	–	–	–	–

Figure 1.23. Complete distinctive feature classification of the sounds of Spanish at the broad phonetic level.

In fact, it seems to me that only two levels of representation
in phonology are significant: the level of representation which
characterizes entries in the lexicon (lexical matrices) and the
level of representation which expresses the 'instructions sent
from the central nervous system to the speech apparatus'
(narrow phonetic representation).

2. Syllable structure has not received much attention in
generative phonological studies. For a good discussion of
Spanish syllable structure, see Hooper (1972). Generally, a
single consonant between two vowels becomes a part of the
syllable which follows it and thus does not close the syllable
which precedes it: [ma-lo], [pe-ro], [pa-to]. If a consonant
cluster occurs at syllable boundary, the cluster will form a
part of a syllable which follows if it is a cluster which can begin a word; otherwise, the cluster will be divided and the first
consonant will close the preceding syllable. Clusters which can
begin words are those which consist of an obstruent followed
by an l or an r: blanco 'white', drama 'play'. Therefore abro
'I open' is divided thus: [a-bro]; however, tengo 'I have' is
divided [tęn-go] and the first syllable is closed, thus lowering
the /e/.

3. The difference between [i] in [si] sí 'yes' and [į] in
[utįl] útil 'useful', is not as great as the difference between
English /i/ and /ɨ/ in beet and bit, respectively. Moreover,
the vowel nucleus of beet contains, in addition to the vowel,
an off-glide which is absent in bit. The phonemic contrast
between English /i/ and /ɨ/ is best described by marking the
/i/ of beet [+ tense] and the /ɨ/ of bit [- tense] (see SPE:68).

4. Spanish palatalized a is nowhere near as far forward as
English a in cat, which is [- back].

5. Harris (1970) discusses the conditions under which these
glides may occur. The word 'potentially' in my description
should be taken to mean that, given a fast enough speech style
and the appropriate environment, any vowel can become a glide.

6. These are not the best comparisons which might be made.
One should actually only compare the constriction lengths of
sounds having identical manners of articulation (e.g. [n] versus [ŋ]). Navarro does not provide a drawing of [ŋ]; however, it would be reasonable to assume that it has the same
type of constriction as do [t] and [d].

7. In SPE, the feature name [continuant] is retained; however, the distinction drawn is the same one defined here.
Nasals and laterals, which have complete blockage at the primary point of articulation but which have an alternate escape
route are marked [- continuant]. I have changed the name of
the feature because of the terminological absurdity of calling a
nasal a noncontinuant.

8. Figure 1.21 does not include all obstruents cited by
Navarro Tomás In addition, he postulates two lax voiceless
fricatives: [đ] in [birtuđ], and [ƀ] in [esƀelto]. To these,
Harris (1969:44) adds [g̊]° (voiceless [g̊] and a voiced series of

tense stops: [p̪,ṭ,ḵ] [ipnotiko] hipnótico 'hypnotic',
[aṭmosfera] atmósfera 'atmosphere', [teḵniko] téknico 'techni-
cian'. These additional segments will be discussed further in
Section 3.3, which deals with voicing assimilation, and are included in Figure 1.23.

CHAPTER 2

PRINCIPLES OF PHONOLOGICAL ANALYSIS

2.0 Introduction. In Chapter One, the sounds of Spanish were presented and described using a system of distinctive features. The remainder of this book is devoted to a discussion of how these sounds form a system of communication.

This chapter deals with the theoretical principles which underlie work in generative phonology, and which are applied to the analysis of the Spanish sound system in Chapters Three through Six.

2.1 Central questions of phonological research. Linguistic competence is discussed in general terms in the Introduction. Phonological competence, in particular, consists primarily of the ability to recognize the basic phonetic units of communication of a language, and the ability to pronounce each unit correctly in its various environments. The construction of a phonological grammar of a particular language can be seen as the attempt to answer questions such as the following.

(1) Which phonetic segments contrast with which other phonetic segments in a manner which is capable of signalling a difference of meaning? For example, [o] contrasts with [a] as evidenced by the contrast between [yo] 'I' and [ya] 'already'.

(2) Which properties of each segment establish the contrasts referred to in Question (1)? For example, [o] and [a] contrast in that [o] is [- low] and [a] is [+ low].

(3) What sequences of segments are considered to be variant pronunciations of the same utterance? For example, in some dialects, [este] and [ehte] are both realizations of este 'this'.

(4) How is the pronunciation of a given communication unit affected by the environment in which it occurs? For example, in some dialects, the nasal n is always pronounced as a velar [ŋ] (like ng in English sing) in word-final position [koŋ el] con él 'with him'.

43

(5) Are there sound segments which signal a difference in meaning in some cases, but which, in other cases, are simply variant pronunciations of some abstract unit? For example, [k] and [θ] contrast in [kořo] corro 'I run' versus [θořo] zorro 'fox', but in [mediko] medico 'doctor' and [mediθina] medicina 'medicine', the two segments [k] and [θ] are simply variant pronunciations of the final segment of the root which is spelled medic- in the standard orthography. (A more detailed analysis of this alternation is given in Section 4.8.)

(6) What are the representations in terms of which speakers remember vocabulary items and store them for future use? For example, ver 'to see', vista 'sight', visible 'visible', and vidente 'one who sees' are all related. Do speakers store these words as indivisible units or do they store a root which is common to all four words; and if the latter, then what is the representation of the root? This last question, which is at the heart of the abstractness issue, is discussed at greater length in Chapters Four and Six.

2.2 The phoneme. Central to these six questions is the idea of the 'phoneme' as an abstract unit of communication which may be manifested by different phonetic segments under differing conditions. An important analytic device which is used in order to determine whether two segments are manifestations of the same phoneme or are manifestations of two different phonemes, is the 'minimal pair test'. A minimal pair is a pair of utterances which differ only with respect to the segments under investigation. Thus [yo] 'I' and [ya] 'already' constitute a minimal pair, and show that [o] and [a] must be assigned to different phonemes. The sequences [este] and [ehte] (the latter of which occurs in Andalusian and certain American dialects) might be used to determine whether or not Spanish has a phonemic [s] versus [h] contrast. Since [este] and [ehte] both mean 'this', the conclusion is that [s] and [h] are manifestations of the same phoneme.

The theory of generative phonology shares with structural phonemics this basic notion of phonemic contrast and the related functional test of the minimal pair. However, there are important differences in the precise definition of phonemic contrast within each theory. The most important difference is that phonemic representations in generative phonology are frequently more abstract than the phonemic representations of American structural phonemics. In an American structuralist analysis, the sounds of a language are classified as manifestations of one phoneme or another, and Question (1) of the previous section is thus answered. Questions (2) and (3) are also answered to varying degrees. However, the answers given to Question (4) by American structural linguists are frequently inadequate, due to their adherence to certain strict conditions governing phonemic analyses. For a thorough discussion of this point, see Chomsky (1964). This is illustrated in Section 3.1.1.1.

Furthermore, Questions (5) and (6) are rarely answered by American structuralists because of their view that phonemics and morphology are independent branches of linguistics.

Because of the classificatory nature of American structural phonemic analyses, this school of phonemics is sometimes called 'taxonomic phonemics', and because of the separation of morphology from phonemics, it is sometimes called 'autonomous phonemics'. The phonology of a generative grammar is frequently called 'systematic phonemics'. Because of the merger of phonemics and morphology, and because of the application of less stringent conditions governing phonemic analyses, systematic phonemic representations tend to be more abstract than the phonemic representations given by structuralists.

2.3 **Systematic phonemic representations.** In Chapter One, the phonetic properties of each Spanish sound segment were characterized in terms of a set of feature specifications. The phonetic representation of a given word or sentence is a string consisting of the feature values of each segment in that word or sentence. The representation takes the form of a matrix, as shown in Figure 2.1, which is the phonetic representation of the word estado. This phonetic representation describes the physical properties of each segment. The analytic device that specifies which of these properties are essential to the use and interpretation of an utterance is the 'systematic phonemic representation'. This representation consists of a sequence of phonemes, also expressed as a matrix, and it differs from the phonetic representation in a number of ways, as illustrated in Figure 2.2.

Figure 2.1. Phonetic representation of the word estado.

	e	s	t	a	d	o
cns	–	+	+	–	+	–
syl	+	–	–	+	–	+
nas	–	–	–	–	–	–
lat	–	–	–	–	–	–
son	+	–	–	+	–	+
ant	–	–	+	–	+	–
low	–	–	–	+	–	–
back	–	–	–	+	–	+
high	–	–	–	–	–	–
rnd	–	–	–	–	–	+
cor	–	+	+	–	+	–
tns	+	+	+	+	–	+
ocl	–	–	+	–	–	–
ins	–	–	+	–	–	–
den	–	–	+	–	+	–
voi	+	–	–	+	+	+

Figure 2.2. Phonemic representation of the word <u>estado</u>.

	s	t	a	d	o
cns	+	+	-	+	-
syl					
nas					
lat					
son	-	-		-	
ant	-	+		+	
low			+		-
back	-				+
high					-
rnd					
cor		+		+	
tns	+	+		-	
ocl	-	+		+	
ins					
den					
voi					

In the first place, many 'plus' or 'minus' values are omitted from the systematic phonemic representation, in order to indicate that the information represented by those 'plus' or 'minus' values is redundant or predictable. That is, it can automatically be deduced from certain other 'plus' or 'minus' values which are included in the matrix. The feature values which are included in the phonemic matrix are those which express the contrastive properties of each segment. In this way, the phonemic matrix provides the answer to Question (2). For example, the [- syllabic] specifications have been omitted from the systematic phonemic representations of /s/, /t/, and /d/ in Figure 2.2. Examination of the chart of Spanish sounds given in Chapter One (Figure 1.23), shows that in Spanish all [+ cns] segments are [- syl]; therefore, these [- syl] specifications are always redundant and are omitted from all phonemic representations.

Secondly, certain features may have the opposite 'plus' or 'minus' value in the phonetic and phonemic matrices. For example, the /d/ of <u>estado</u> is marked [+ occlusive] in the systematic phonemic representation (Figure 2.2), but [- occlusive] in the phonetic representation (Figure 2.1). Although the basic pronunciation of /d/ is as a stop, the phoneme /d/ is subject to a modification which reverses the value of the feature [occlusive] in certain contexts. This phenomenon is discussed in detail in Section 3.2.

In addition to differences involving the internal feature composition of individual segments, the phonetic and phonemic representations may contain different segments. For example,

the initial [e] of <u>estado</u> is completely predictable, and is thus
devoid of any communicative value.   This [e] is therefore not
present in the phonemic matrix for the word.

Thus, while the phonetic representation is constructed so as
to express all the finer details of pronunciation, the phonemic
representation includes all and only the information which the
analyst believes to be representative of the sound system of the
language.

These two levels of representation, the phonemic level and the
phonetic level, are related to each other by a set of rules which
take the phonemic representation of an utterance as input and
produce the phonetic representation of that utterance as output.
These rules constitute the formal rules of pronunciation of a
language, and are formulated as demonstrated in the following
section.

2.4   The format of a phonological rule.   Each phonological
rule consists of three parts, as demonstrated in Rule (2.1).
The input is labelled (a), the output (b), and the context (c).

(a) input   (b) output   (c) context
(2.1)   [+ Feature-1] ----→ [+ Feature-2] / ___ [+ Feature-3]

In Rule (2.1), the first part, (a), is the input to the rule.
In the input, the class of segments to which the rule applies
is specified.   In this case, the class of segments to which the
rule applies is all those segments which are specified positively
with respect to [Feature-1], which can be any of the phonological features discussed in Chapter One.   In the next part, the
output (b), the feature specifications which are to be applied
to all input segments are listed.   In this case, the rule states
that all segments which are specified positively with respect to
[Feature-1], acquire a positive specification for [Feature-2] as
well.   Part (c) is the context, and indicates what other properties must be present for the rule to apply.   In this case, the
context part states that the rule only applies to a segment which
is followed by a segment specified positively for [Feature-3].

In this rule, the arrow and the diagonal slash serve to separate the parts of the rule.   The arrow (----→) can be read
'becomes', and the slash (/) can be read 'if'.   The underscore
(___) indicates the position of the input segment within the context.   Thus the entire rule (2.1) can be read as follows: 'Any
segment which is plus [Feature-1], becomes plus [Feature-2],
if it is followed by a segment which is plus [Feature-3].

An actual example is given as Rule (2.2), which reads as
follows: 'Any segment which is minus [consonantal] and plus
[high] (i.e. /i/ or /u/) becomes minus [syllabic] (i.e. [j] or
[w], respectively) if it is followed by another vowel (in the
context "before vowel")'.

(2.2) $\begin{bmatrix} - \text{ cns} \\ + \text{ high} \end{bmatrix}$ ----→ [- syl] / ___ [+ syl]

Three facts about the way rules of this sort are to be interpreted must be made clear at this point.

(1) If a feature is not mentioned in the input of a rule (to the left of the arrow), then it is irrelevant to the decision as to whether or not the rule applies to a given segment. Thus Rule (2.2) will apply to the segment /u/ (as represented in Figure 2.3) because the two conditions are met (i.e. the segment is both plus [syllabic] and plus [high]). Rule (2.2) will not, however, apply to /o/ (see Figure 2.3) because the segment /o/ is [- high] and the rule stipulates that it can only apply to [+ high] segments.

Figure 2.3. Feature complexes of /u/ and /o/.

/u/	/o/
$\begin{bmatrix} + \text{ syl} \\ - \text{ low} \\ + \text{ back} \\ + \text{ high} \\ + \text{ rnd} \end{bmatrix}$	$\begin{bmatrix} + \text{ syl} \\ - \text{ low} \\ + \text{ back} \\ - \text{ high} \\ + \text{ rnd} \end{bmatrix}$

(2) If a feature is not mentioned in the output section of a rule, then its value will not be affected by the rule. That is, Rule (2.2) will apply to both /i/ and /u/ and the outputs will be [j] and [w], respectively. As shown in Figure 2.4, only the specification for the feature [syllabic] is changed in each case.

Figure 2.4. Feature complexes of /u/ and /w/ and of /i/ and [j] showing the effects of Rule (2.2).

/u/ $\begin{bmatrix} + \text{ syl} \\ - \text{ low} \\ + \text{ back} \\ + \text{ high} \\ + \text{ rnd} \end{bmatrix}$	/i/ $\begin{bmatrix} + \text{ syl} \\ - \text{ low} \\ - \text{ back} \\ + \text{ high} \\ - \text{ rnd} \end{bmatrix}$
[w] $\begin{bmatrix} - \text{ syl} \\ - \text{ low} \\ + \text{ back} \\ + \text{ high} \\ + \text{ rnd} \end{bmatrix}$	[j] $\begin{bmatrix} - \text{ syl} \\ - \text{ low} \\ - \text{ back} \\ + \text{ high} \\ - \text{ rnd} \end{bmatrix}$

(3) The environment bar is used typically in the following three ways:

(a) . . . / ___ [+ Feature-3]

(b) . . . / [+ Feature-3] ___

(c) . . . /
$$\begin{bmatrix} \\ + \text{Feature-3} \end{bmatrix}$$

Use (a) is identical to the usage illustrated in Rule (2.1), and, as explained earlier, means 'if followed by a segment which is specified positively for [Feature-3]'. Use (b) means 'if preceded by a segment which is specified positively for [Feature-3]', and use (c) means 'if the segment to which the rule is to apply is itself specified positively for [Feature -3]'.

Given use (c), Rule (2.2) might be reformulated as Rule (2.2').

(2.2') [- cns] ----➤ [- syl] /
$$\begin{bmatrix} \\ + \text{high} \end{bmatrix}$$ [+ syl]

Rule (2.2') states that 'any segment which is minus [consonantal] becomes minus [syllabic] if it is plus [high] and if it is followed by a segment which is plus [syllabic]. Although the formulations and the prose translations differ, Rules (2.2) and (2.2') apply to the exact same segments.

2.5 Abbreviatory devices. As mentioned in Section 0.3.2, the theoretical framework specifies ways in which related rules can be combined with each other. There are numerous abbreviatory conventions which are used in phonological rules. The majority of these are explained in subsequent chapters as they are needed for the treatment of Spanish phenomena. However, one convention, which is used extensively, is explained here.

Rule (2.3), which is related to Rule (2.2), is also a rule of Spanish.

(2.3)
$$\begin{bmatrix} + \text{syl} \\ + \text{high} \end{bmatrix}$$ ----➤ [- syl] / [+ syl] ___

Rule (2.3) states that a high vowel becomes a glide if it occurs immediately after another vowel. What is expressed in Rules (2.2) and (2.3) is a single phenomenon, not two: a high vowel becomes a glide if it is next to another vowel. Therefore a single rule must be formulated which expresses this phenomenon in a unitary manner. This is done by combining Rule (2.2) and Rule (2.3) into a single rule, which is given as Rule (2.4).

(2.4) $\begin{bmatrix} - \text{ cns} \\ + \text{ high} \end{bmatrix}$ ----→ [- syl] / $\begin{cases} \underline{\hspace{1cm}} & [+ \text{ syl}] \quad \text{(a)} \\ [+ \text{ syl}] & \underline{\hspace{1cm}} \quad \text{(b)} \end{cases}$

In Rule (2.4), the braces enclose alternative environments.
By convention, Rule (2.4) is expanded into (2.2) and (2.3).
The use of the braces notation allows any two rules which share
certain elements and which do similar things to be combined
into a single rule. As mentioned earlier, a number of other
abbreviatory devices (including a device that makes it possible
to simplify Rule (2.4) even further), are introduced as they
are needed.

2.6 The order of application of phonological rules. Throughout this book, the rules discussed are presumed to be ordered.
That is, they apply one after another, and the output of one
rule is the input to the next rule. For example, Rule (2.4)
might be followed by Rule (2.5).

(2.5) $\begin{bmatrix} - \text{ syl} \\ - \text{ cns} \end{bmatrix}$ ----→ $\begin{bmatrix} + \text{ cns} \\ - \text{ son} \end{bmatrix}$ / - \underline{\hspace{1cm}}

Rule (2.5) states that a segment which is minus [syllabic]
and minus [consonantal] (a glide) becomes plus [consonantal]
and minus [sonorant] (an obstruent) if it is syllable-initial.
The effect of this rule is to convert the glides formed by Rule
(2.4), and perhaps other glides as well, into obstruents whenever they occur in syllable-initial position. The application of
Rule (2.4) and Rule (2.5) to words such as huevo and hierba
is shown in Figure 2.5. Rule (2.4) converts the high vowels
to glides, and Rule (2.5) converts these glides to obstruents.
The actual relationship between these two rules is somewhat
more complicated than suggested here. Only some glides are
subject to Rule (2.5). These derivations are discussed in detail in Sections 3.5 and 3.6, and again in Section 4.7.

Figure 2.5. Derivations of huevo and yerba showing the
effect of ordered rules.

	/u e b o/	/i e r b a/
Rule (2.4)	w	j
Rule (2.5)	ǥ ʷ	y
	[ǥʷ e ƀ o]	[y e r ƀ a]

The ordering hypothesis followed in this book is the subject
of considerable discussion at the time of this writing. Other
hypotheses which have been advanced recently are (1) the
Random-Sequential hypothesis, which states that rules apply in
a random order, and (2) the Simultaneous Rule Application

hypothesis, which states that all rules apply simultaneously to the phonemic representation yielding the phonetic representation. In either of these cases, each rule must be formulated so that its correct application does not depend upon the order of application of the entire set.

Furthermore, among adherents of ordered rules, there is a difference of opinion as to whether or not the order of application of the rules of a language must be explicitly specified (for example, by associating a number with each rule). This point of view is known as the theory of 'extrinsic ordering'. According to the opposite point of view (sometimes called the theory of 'intrinsic ordering'), the order of a set of rules follows automatically from the nature of the rules themselves. For example, according to this latter view, Rule (2.4) naturally precedes Rule (2.5) because Rule (2.4) creates segments which are possible inputs to Rule (2.5).

The assumption that rules apply in a determined order, which is followed in this book, is the standard generative view. I adhere to it because, in my opinion, proponents of other hypotheses have never achieved results as satisfactory as those of Harris (1969), which is the first major generative treatment of Spanish phonology, and which depends heavily upon ordered rules. As shown in the next section, Rules (2.4) and (2.5) illustrate rather well the usefulness of ordered rules. In the derivation of huevo, for example, Rule (2.4) converts the /u/ to the glide [w] and Rule (2.5) converts the glide [w] to the obstruent [g̊ʷ]. However, the rules are independent of each other and cannot be combined into a single rule. There are instances of [w] which do not undergo Rule (2.5) because they are not syllable-initial, e.g. the [w] of [pweɖo] puedo 'I can'.

With regard to the second issue, I take the point of view that the rules are largely ordered intrinsically, but that extrinsic ordering is a valid analytic device available to the linguist when it is needed.

2.7 Evaluation and comparison of phonemic analyses. As explained in Section 0.4.3, a theoretical framework is capable of explaining linguistic phenomena, i.e. meeting the highest level of adequacy, if and only if, the metatheory includes an automatic way of determining which of two competing analyses, both of which are compatible with the data, is superior, i.e. expresses the correct generalizations about the language in question.

As an example, consider three possible analyses of Spanish words which begin with [g̊ʷe] (huevo, hueso, etc.).

Analysis (1).

Phonemic Representations: /webo/ /weso/

Rule (2.5) $\begin{bmatrix} - \text{ syl} \\ - \text{ cns} \end{bmatrix} \dashrightarrow \begin{bmatrix} + \text{ cns} \\ - \text{ son} \end{bmatrix} / - \underline{\quad}$

Phonetic Representations: [ǧ$^\text{W}$ebo] [ǧ$^\text{W}$eso]

Analysis (2).

Phonemic Representations: /uebo/ /ueso/

Rule (2.6) $\begin{bmatrix} - \text{ cns} \\ + \text{ high} \end{bmatrix} \dashrightarrow \begin{bmatrix} - \text{ syl} \\ + \text{ cns} \\ - \text{ son} \end{bmatrix} / - \underline{\quad} [+ \text{ syl}]$

Phonetic Representations: [ǧ$^\text{W}$ebo] [ǧ$^\text{W}$eso]

Analysis (3).

Phonemic Representations: /uebo/ /ueso/

Rule (2.4) $\begin{bmatrix} - \text{ cns} \\ + \text{ high} \end{bmatrix} \dashrightarrow [- \text{ syl}] / \begin{Bmatrix} \underline{\qquad} \ [+ \text{ syl}] \\ [+ \text{ syl}] \ \underline{\qquad} \end{Bmatrix}$

Rule (2.5) $\begin{bmatrix} - \text{ syl} \\ - \text{ cns} \end{bmatrix} \dashrightarrow \begin{bmatrix} + \text{ cns} \\ - \text{ son} \end{bmatrix} / - \underline{\quad}$

Phonetic Representations: [ǧ$^\text{W}$ebo] [ǧ$^\text{W}$eso]

As demonstrated by the phonetic representations included in all three analyses, all of them yield the same results. Thus no decision among them is possible on the basis of compatibility with the data. All three analyses meet observational adequacy. A choice among the three analyses must be made by applying the criterion of descriptive adequacy: Which analysis best expresses the correct generalizations concerning the sound system of Spanish?

It must be noted in passing that none of these analyses is the one which is ultimately selected as correct in this book (see Section 4.7). However, the three analyses can still be contrasted with each other, in order to determine which one is superior to the other two.

Analysis (1) expresses the phonemic representations of these words in terms of a glide phoneme, thereby establishing a glide phoneme independent of the high vowel phoneme. However,

glides and vowels are not in contrast with each other in this
environment--there are no minimal pairs such as [weso] versus
[ueso]. Therefore, there is no basis upon which to posit an
independent glide phoneme in these representations.[1]

Analysis (2) corrects the error mentioned in connection with
Analysis (1), by representing these words with initual /u/.
These instances of /u/ are then converted to [g̶ʷ] by Rule
(2.6), which is a combination of Rules (2.4) and (2.5) into a
single rule. However, as suggested earlier, Rules (2.4) and
(2.5) are independent of each other and cannot be combined.
In effect, Rule (2.6) is an ad hoc rule, formulated solely for
the purpose of accounting for the phonetic forms of words such
as huevo and hueso.

Analysis (3) uses two rules to accomplish what Analysis (2)
does with one rule, and therefore at first glance, Analysis (2)
might be considered to be superior. However, Rule (2.4) must
be included in any grammar of Spanish which is to meet even
observational adequacy, since there are instances of [w] and
[j] which are syllable-internal. These syllable-internal glides
must be derived from vowels, and the rule which accomplishes
this is Rule (2.4). Examples are [kwota] from /kuota/ and
[rad̶jo] from /radio/.

Since Rule (2.4) must be included in any grammar of Spanish,
the question at issue is whether the conversion of the initial
segments of words like hueso and huevo to obstruents should
be considered an independent phenomenon, not related to the
conversion of syllable-internal high vowels to glides. From the
standpoint of making the appropriate generalizations about Spanish, it seems that these two phenomena should be analyzed as
different manifestations of a single phenomenon; namely, the
loss of the feature [+ syllabic]. That is, all the high vowels
under discussion become [- syllabic] when they occur in contact with another vowel. Therefore Rule (2.4) should express
this general fact by applying to both the cuota, radio type of
word and the hueso, huevo type of word. Once Rule (2.4) has
applied to hueso and huevo, Rule (2.5) is the only way to complete the conversion to [g̶ʷ]. Therefore, we conclude that the
goal of describing the phonological properties of Spanish is
more fully met by an analysis which includes Rules (2.4) and
(2.6), and that Analysis (3) is superior to the other two.

2.7.1 **The simplicity metric.** The device used in generative
phonology to measure analyses mechanically and compare them
is the simplicity metric. The simplicity metric is, in effect, a
formula which can be used to assign to a particular analysis a
'cost'. Two analyses can then be compared and the one with
the lower cost is deemed to be superior. If the method of
determining cost has been defined properly, calculations of
lowest cost must always agree with judgments of relative descriptive adequacy such as those made in the preceding section in conjunction with Analyses (1), (2), and (3).

It is important to emphasize the fact that the ultimate decision as to which of two or more competing analyses is the best
one, is an empirical decision. The choice of the best analysis
is made by examining the relevant data and applying arguments
such as those advanced in favor of Analysis (3) in the preceding section. Usually, an analysis is considered better because
it expresses a phenomenon in more general terms. However,
mechanical economy alone is not an indication of superiority.
That is, one does not evaluate analyses in terms of some arbitrarily determined simplicity metric (formula for calculating
cost). On the contrary, one evaluates a proposed simplicity
metric (formula) by seeing if it consistently selects analyses
which have been judged superior on empirical grounds.[2]
The basic formula usually used to measure economy is to
count the number of feature specifications used in the analysis.
Thus the most economical analysis is the one which makes use
of the smallest number of feature specifications in the lexicon
and in the rules. Although this calculation of economy seems
quite simple and straightforward, it must be remembered that
any abbreviatory device which is used to combine two or more
rules into one, will have an impact upon the total number of
feature specifications used in the analysis. Thus, one important
goal of research in theoretical phonology is the formulation of
abbreviatory devices which improve the correlation between
mechanical economy and true descriptive generality. If the
economy made possible by a proposed abbreviatory device does
correlate with descriptive generality, then the device is accepted and becomes a part of the metatheory. If, however, a
proposed abbreviatory device makes possible a false economy,
which has no descriptive basis, then the proposed device is
rejected.

2.7.2 **Application of the simplicity metric to Analyses (1),
(2), and (3).** As shown in detail in Chapter Five, many features can be left unspecified in lexical matrices because they
are predictable from the environment. Thus Rule (2.4) does
not actually convert a vowel to a glide but rather accepts as
input a nonconsonantal segment which is unspecified for the
feature [syllabic] and further specifies that segment as a
glide. Thus, although the phonemic representations of Analyses (1) and (2) appear to be equally complex, these representations are actually shorthand versions of the actual representations, which are expressed in terms of features; the phonemic
representations of Analysis (2) are, in fact, unspecified for the
feature [syllabic], whereas those of Analysis (1) are specified
as [- syllabic]. Thus the rule used in Analysis (2) makes
possible a considerable saving of feature specifications in the
lexicon, and hence Analysis (2) is more economical than Analysis (1).
Regarding Analyses (2) and (3), Rule (2.4) is required in
any grammar of Spanish, regardless of whether Analysis (2) or

(3) is chosen for the description of the cases under discussion. Since Rule (2.5) is less costly than Rule (2.6), Analysis (3) is less costly than Analysis (2).

Since these mechanical computations of cost correspond to the descriptive adequacy judgments made earlier, Analysis (3) was judged to be the best on descriptive grounds; and it is also the simplest mechanically--it can be concluded that the simplicity metric, insofar as it has been discussed thus far, is supported by the data and the analyses just discussed.

2.8   The subcomponents of a generative phonology. The complete phonological description of a language is given by a lexicon which contains a lexical representation for every lexical item in the language, and a set of rules which relates the syntactic surface structure of a sentence to its narrow phonetic representation.   In this book, the phonological rules are assumed to be grouped into subcomponents as illustrated in Figure 2.6.

Figure 2.6.   Subcomponents of a generative phonology.

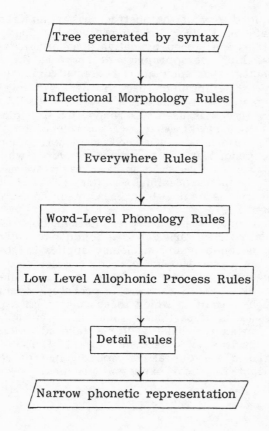

The 'Detail Rules', which serve to specify the most narrow phonetic details of pronunciation, have been discussed in Chapter One.

The 'Low Level Allophonic Process Rules' are treated in Chapter Three. These rules are the ones which most resemble the rules posited by taxonomic phonemicists, and serve to relate the sounds of Spanish to an inventory of phonemes. The 'Word-level Phonology Rules' are more abstract than the 'Low Level Allophonic Process Rules' and frequently involve alternations such as the one mentioned in Section 2.1 in connection with words such as médico and medicina.

The 'Everywhere Rules' constitute an exception to the principle of ordered rules explained in Section 2.6. The Everywhere Rules apply initially to an utterance as it emerges from the morphological subcomponent. From this point downward in the derivation, an Everywhere Rule applies whenever its structural description is met.

The Inflectional Morphology Rules are the most abstract of those discussed in this book and serve to spell out inflectional endings of nouns, adjectives, and verbs.

2.9 A variable theory of the abstractness of lexical representations. The standard theory of generative phonology holds that lexical entries are stored by native speakers in terms of representations which are appropriate to serve as the input to the entire phonological component as represented in Figure 2.6.

More recently, some linguists (e.g. Hooper 1973 and Halle 1974) have suggested that some rules may not actually apply to a word every time it is used. Perhaps, for example, a native speaker may have knowledge of the rule which accounts for the [k] ~ [θ] alternation in médico--medicina, and may apply that knowledge in learning to pronounce words which are new to him. However, that same speaker may store médico as /mediko/ and medicina as /mediθina/ rather than with some common stem-final consonant (which is represented by c in the standard orthography).

The variable theory of lexical representations holds that storage of lexical entries varies from individual to individual. Every speaker, no doubt, subconsciously applies the Detail Rules and the Low Level Allophonic Process Rules to a word each time he uses it. However, in the case of the rules of Chapters Four, Five, and Six, there is probably considerable variation as to the extent to which these rules form a part of the working grammars of particular speakers. The lexical entries of some speakers probably do not take advantage of some of the regularities expressed in these chapters. Thus, the lexical entries of some speakers probably include redundant specifications which this book expresses in rules.

NOTES

1. It is shown in Section 3.5.1.4.1 that it is necessary in some instances to mark the vowel versus glide distinction at the phonemic level. However, the cases involved do not alter the present argument.

2. There has often been confusion concerning the relationship between the simplicity metric and specific analyses. One can argue that a specific analysis is superior because it is simpler only if one is completely confident of the correctness of the simplicity metric. Furthermore, the correctness of a proposed simplicity metric must be proven empirically, with reference to particular analyses. For a clear statement of this relationship, see Chomsky and Halle (1968:330-331).

CHAPTER 3

THE SYSTEMATIC PHONEMES OF SPANISH

3.0 Introduction. In this chapter, the systematic phonemes
of Spanish are identified and the sounds which can occur as
manifestations of each phoneme are specified along with the en-
vironment(s) in which each sound occurs. Rules are formulated
which relate each phoneme to its various manifestations. The
rules discussed are generally considered Low Level Allophonic
Process Rules; and, for the most part, they are accepted as
valid by linguists who differ as to how abstract phonological
representations should be. The general properties of these
rules are the following: (1) each rule changes few features of
the segments to which it applies, (2) each rule applies across
a word boundary as well as within words, (3) each rule is subject to a certain amount of variation (see Section 3.0.1), (4)
all of the rules can be ordered near the end of the phonological component, and (5) all of the rules are productive; that is,
they apply to new words which are coined or borrowed from
other languages.

Since each of the rules discussed in this chapter applies
across a word boundary as well as within words, this fact is
not expressed in the environment part of each rule. It seems
incorrect to include an optional word boundary in the environment part of each of a set of rules when the application of the
rules across a word boundary is a general property of the set.
(See Harris 1969:58ff. for discussion.) If all the rules which
apply across a word boundary can be ordered together near the
end of the phonological component, then the desired result can
be obtained (as suggested in Harris 1969:59), by deleting, at
the appropriate place in the derivation, the symbol # from the
representation of an utterance. If this ordering is not possible, then the same result might be obtained by associating with
each rule a label, such as 'AP' (for 'Allophonic Process') which
automatically entails the five properties attributed to these rules
in the preceding paragraph.

The inventory of the systematic phonemes of Spanish, and a
partially filled in matrix of their feature specifications, are presented in Figure 3.1. However, it is not possible to construct
a matrix of the sort presented in Figure 3.1 in such a way that
each phoneme is displayed exactly as it appears in every morpheme in which it occurs. This is due to the fact that a given
phoneme may require one set of feature specifications in certain
environments and another (larger or smaller) set of feature
specifications in other environments. For example, Spanish
/r̃/ must be distinguished from /r/ in medial position, e.g.
[per̃o] perro 'dog' versus [pero] pero 'but'. This distinction
is established by marking /r̃/ [+ tense] and /r/ [- tense] in
medial position. However, it is not necessary to maintain this
distinction in initial position since only [r̃] occurs in initial
position and therefore, there is no phonemic contrast in initial
position of [r̃] versus [r]. Accordingly, the feature [tense] is
not specified for initial r, that is, the specification is left blank,
or marked ∅.
   In developing Figure 3.1, I have proceeded as follows. I
have posited a phoneme for every segment class which occurs
in the lexicon in contrast with another segment class, and I
have constructed the most efficient matrix possible[1] for the
classification of these phonemes. Figure 3.1 requires the
following clarifications.
   (1) Although only five vowel phonemes are listed in Figure
3.1, nonphonetic distinctions must be made between vowels
which diphthongize under stress and those which do not, e.g.
poder 'to be able', puedo 'I can' versus comer 'to eat', como
'I eat' and a feature must be posited to account for stress
assignment, e.g. [sábana] sábana 'sheet' versus [sabána]
sabana 'grassy plain'. These phenomena, and the features
involved, are discussed in Chapter Four.
   (2) Glides appear as systematic phonemes. This is because
the distinction between a glide and a high vowel must be specified in the lexicon in some cases, e.g. the u of baúl 'trunk'
must be explicitly marked [+ syllabic] in the lexicon. This is
discussed in detail in Section 3.5.1.4.1.1.
   In this chapter, the following phenomena are discussed: (1)
nasal and lateral assimilation (Section 3.1), (2) alternation of
lax stops and fricatives (Section 3.2), (3) obstruent voicing
assimilation (Section 3.3), (4) laxing of vowels (Section 3.4),
(5) formation of glides (Section 3.5), and (6) spirantization of
glides (Section 3.6). As the exposition of these phenomena
progresses, certain theoretical questions which arise are discussed, and tentative answers which seem to be in conformity
with the Spanish data are suggested.

   3.0.1 Variation. Generative grammars have, from the out-
set, distinguished between obligatory and optional rules. An
optional rule may be applied or not applied, and the result of
the presence of an obligatory rule in a grammar is the

Figure 3.1. Feature specifications required for the classification of the systematic phonemes of Spanish.

	i	e	a	o	u	j	w	r	r̃	l	l̃	m	n	ñ	p	t	ĉ	k	b	d	y	g	f	θ	s	x	
[cns]	−	−	−	−	−	−	−	+	+	+	+	+	+	+	+	+	+	+	+	+	+	+	+	+	+	+	[cns]
[syl]	+	+	+	+	+	−	−	−	−	−	−	−	−	−	−	−	−	−	−	−	−	−	−	−	−	−	[syl]
[nas]								−	−	−	−	+	+	+	−	−	−	−	−	−	−	−	−	−	−	−	[nas]
[lat]								−	−	+	+	−	−	−													[lat]
[son]	+	+	+	+	+	+	+	+	+	+	+	+	+	+	−	−	−	−	−	−	−	−	−	−	−	−	[son]
[ant]								+	+	+	−	+	+	−	+	+	−	−	+	+	−	−	+	+	+	−	[ant]
[low]	−	−	+	−	−																						[low]
[back]	−	−	+	+	+	−	+											+				+				+	[back]
[high]	+	−	−	−	+	+	+				+			+			+	+			+	+				+	[high]
[rnd]	−	−	−	+	+	−	+																				[rnd]
[cor]								+	+	+	+	−	+	+	−	+	+	−	−	+	+	−	−	+	+	−	[cor]
[tns]								−	+						+	+	+	+	−	−	−	−	+	+	+	+	[tns]
[ocl]								−	−						+	+	+	+	+	+	−	+	−	−	−	−	[ocl]
[ins]									+																		[ins]
[den]																+				+				+			[den]
[voi]								+	+	+	+	+	+	+	−	−	−	−	+	+	+	+	−	−	−	−	[voi]

establishment of two or more stylistic variants of the same
utterance. Formerly, these variants were said to be in 'free
variation' with each other. However, work in sociolinguistics
(see, for example, Labov 1966) has shown that variation is sel-
dom, if ever, 'free', and that it is possible to investigate and
describe the factors which contribute to the application or non-
application of a particular rule.

One of the factors is described in Harris (1969:7). Harris
describes four speech styles: largo, andante, allegretto, and
presto. These styles are defined in terms of speed and precision of speaking. In many instances, it is possible to identify
other factors which operate in conjunction with precision, and
even to establish a hierarchy of importance among the factors.

In this study, variation is not analyzed in detail. However,
in many instances the rules are variable, and in one or two
instances the factors which condition a rule can be identified.

3.1 Nasal and lateral assimilation. A nasal which is followed
directly by another consonant becomes homorganic with that
consonant, i.e. the nasal assimilates to the point of articulation
of the following consonant. This assimilation always takes place
within words. It also takes place across a word boundary unless a phonetic phrase boundary (pause) occurs between the
two words.

Laterals also assimilate to the point of articulation of a
following consonant provided the consonant has a point of
articulation which a lateral can assume, i.e. provided it is
dental, alveolar, palato-alveolar, or palatal.

These two phenomena are discussed in Sections 3.1.1 to 3.1.3.
In conjunction with the formulation of a rule to account for
nasal and lateral assimilation, four theoretical matters arise.
(1) The condition of bi-uniqueness, frequently maintained by
taxonomic phonemicists, is seen to be incorrect (Section
3.1.1.1). (2) The need is shown for a formal equivalent of
the term 'homorganic' (Section 3.1.1.2). (3) Some further evidence is provided for the definition of the feature [occlusive]
presented in Chapter One (Section 3.1.2.1). (4) A special use
of redundancy rules is suggested to account for the fact that
lateral assimilation applies over a more restricted range of points
of articulation than does nasal assimilation (Section 3.1.3.1).

Nasal and lateral assimilation are first discussed separately
(Sections 3.1.1 and 3.1.2), and then a single rule is formulated
to account for both phenomena (Section 3.1.3).

3.1.1 Nasal assimilation. The nasal consonants of Spanish,
as described in Chapter One, are displayed in Figure 3.2.

The nasals [m], [n], and [ñ] contrast phonemically in intervocalic position, e.g. cama 'bed', cana 'white hair', caña 'cane',
and are realizations of the three nasal phonemes /m/, /n/, and
/ñ/, respectively.

Figure 3.2. Distinctive feature classification of the nasal consonant phones of Spanish.

	m	m̰	n̪	n	n̂	ñ	ŋ
[high]	–	–	–	–	+	+	+
[back]	–	–	–	–	–	–	+
[ant]	+	+	+	+	–	–	–
[cor]	–	–	+	+	+	–	–
[den]	–	+	+	–	–	–	–

However, in a sequence of the type [+ nas]⁀[+ cns], there is no phonemic contrast between nasals since the point of articulation of the nasal is conditioned by the point of articulation of the following consonant. This is illustrated by the following realizations of the indefinite article /un/ un 'a'.

[um beso] un beso 'a kiss'
[um̰ fenomeno] un fenómeno 'a phenomenon'
[un̪ tiro] un tiro 'a shot'
[un niño] un niño 'a child'
[un̂ ĉiko] un chico 'a boy'
[uñ yate] un yate 'a yacht'
[uŋ gato] un gato 'a cat'

3.1.1.1 Nasal assimilation and the taxonomic phonemic level. The situation described in the previous section, phonemic contrast between nasals in one environment, and the absence of any phonemic contrast in another, provides strong evidence against the taxonomic phonemicists' conception of phonemic representations. As explained in Section 2.2, the taxonomic level of phonemic representation is considerably less abstract than the phonemic level envisioned in a generative analysis, the systematic phonemic level.

In Chomsky (1964:91ff.), this difference is characterized in terms of a number of conditions adhered to, in varying degrees, by American structuralists. It should be pointed out that the desirability of maintaining a close relationship between phonetics and phonemics is shared by both taxonomic phonemicists and generative phonologists. The latter have also explored the possibility of constraining phonological theory in appropriate ways by the use of conditions; see, for example, Postal (1968) and Kiparsky (1968). Although generative phonologists recognize the need for such conditions, it is evident that the particular conditions which characterize taxonomic phonemics are far too strong and produce incorrect results if applied to the analysis of the phonetic and the phonemic distributions of Spanish nasals. In this instance the condition of bi-uniqueness, which stipulates that once a sound has been classified as a manifestation of a given phoneme in a specific

environment, that sound must be represented by the same phoneme wherever it occurs, leads to incorrect results. That is,
since /m/, /n/, and /ñ/ contrast intervocalically (cama 'bed'
versus cana 'white hair' versus caña 'cane'), the condition of
bi-uniqueness requires that any phonetic [m] must be represented phonemically as /m/. Thus, the phrase [um beso]
un beso 'a kiss' must be represented phonemically as /um
beso/, and three phonemic representations of the indefinite
article must be posited: /un, um, uñ/. In order to express
the fact that these three sequences of phonemes all have the
same meaning, taxonomic phonemicists have stated that they are
three 'allomorphs' of the indefinite article un 'a'. However,
given this analysis, in terms of three levels of representation
(the morpheme, the allomorphs represented at the phonemic
level, and the phonetic representations), two rules will be required to account for nasal assimilation: one to relate the n
of the morpheme un to the phonemes /m, n, ñ/ in the allomorphs of un, and another to relate the phoneme /n/ to the
allophones [m̧, ŋ, n, ñ, ŋ]. The problem is that these two
rules express essentially the same fact about Spanish--that
nasals assimilate to a following consonant. Clearly, nasal
assimilation is one phenomenon, not two. Therefore, the theoretical hypothesis which requires it to be analyzed as two phenomena must be incorrect; and the condition of bi-uniqueness
must be rejected.

**3.1.1.2 The need for a formal equivalent of the term 'hom-
organic'.** In the previous section, it is shown that it is not
possible to express nasal assimilation as a unitary phenomenon
within the framework of traditional phonemics. The formulation of a generative rule which expresses the correct generalization also poses a difficulty, but of another sort.

The phenomenon of nasal assimilation was defined informally
in Section 3.2 as follows: a nasal which is followed directly by
another consonant becomes homorganic with that consonant.
The formulation of a rule to express this fact in feature notation, however, is not a simple matter. The usual manner of
expressing assimilatory phenomena of this type is by specifying
agreement of feature specifications using the alpha convention
defined in Section 1.2.2.3.2. Agreement between a nasal and
a following consonant is specified for each point of articulation
feature by the use of a separate Greek letter, as shown in
Rule (3.1).

$$
(3.1) \quad [+ \text{nasal}] \longrightarrow
\begin{bmatrix}
\alpha \text{ high} \\
\beta \text{ back} \\
\gamma \text{ ant} \\
\delta \text{ cor} \\
\varepsilon \text{ den}
\end{bmatrix}
/ \underline{\quad}
\begin{bmatrix}
+ \text{ cns} \\
\alpha \text{ high} \\
\beta \text{ back} \\
\gamma \text{ ant} \\
\delta \text{ cor} \\
\varepsilon \text{ den}
\end{bmatrix}
$$

However, a serious theoretical deficiency is manifested by this rule which must specify five separate feature agreements in order to effect what is essentially the copying of but one factor, the point of articulation, from one segment to another.

In order to make this theoretical deficiency somewhat more explicit, compare Rule (3.1) with the hypothetical case given in Rule (3.2).

$$(3.2) \quad [+ \text{nasal}] \longrightarrow \begin{bmatrix} \alpha \text{ ant} \\ \beta \text{ cor} \\ \delta \text{ voi} \\ \gamma \text{ ocl} \\ \varepsilon \text{ den} \end{bmatrix} / \underline{} \begin{bmatrix} + \text{ cns} \\ \alpha \text{ ant} \\ \beta \text{ cor} \\ \delta \text{ voi} \\ \gamma \text{ ocl} \\ \varepsilon \text{ den} \end{bmatrix}$$

Rule (3.2) is identical to Rule (3.1) except that instead of specifying agreement of the five main points of articulation features, Rule (3.2) specifies agreement of an arbitrarily selected set of features. In spite of the fact that Rule (3.1) expresses a phenomenon common to many languages, and Rule (3.2) expresses a highly unlikely situation, both rules entail the same cost. Therefore, if cost is to be taken seriously as a measure of generality, some change must be introduced to allow the formulation of Rule (3.1) in such a way that it is less costly than Rule (3.2).

Harris (1969:20) discusses this problem and suggests that it should be possible to state an assimilation as in Rule (3.3).

$$(3.3) \quad \text{ASSIMILATE:} \quad \begin{bmatrix} \underline{} \\ 1,n \end{bmatrix} [+ \text{obstr}]$$

However, it is clear that Harris' suggestion should be interpreted as an indication of the direction in which one might search for a solution--not as a technically worked out proposal for new notation. This is so primarily because there are other types of assimilation besides that of the point of articulation, for example, voicing assimilation. Therefore, a formal proposal to implement Harris' suggestion must specify in some way what type of assimilation is involved.

In effect, what is needed is a way to refer to all and only the point of articulation features by a single specification in a rule. The notational convention in Rule (3.4) is designed to accomplish this.

The notation PA (standing for 'point of articulation') constitutes an abbreviation of the unsigned feature complex [high, back, anterior, coronal, dental]. The specification [α PA] shall be expanded, wherever it is used in a rule, as [α high, β back, γ anterior, δ coronal, ε dental]. Thus the notation [α PA], when used in the feature complexes of two segments, indicates that the two segments share all point of articulation features, i.e. have the same point of articulation, or are 'homorganic'.

The rule for nasal assimilation can now be formulated as in Rule (3.4).

$$(3.4) \quad [+ \text{ nasal}] \longrightarrow \alpha \text{ PA } / \underline{\hspace{1cm}} \begin{bmatrix} + \text{ cns} \\ \alpha \text{ PA} \end{bmatrix}$$

Given the convention proposed here, Rule (3.4) will be expanded as Rule (3.1).

This abbreviatory device, then, makes it possible for the point of articulation to be referred to with a single specification and thereby makes it possible to treat the point of articulation copying process inherent in nasal assimilation as a unitary phenomenon.

3.1.2 Lateral assimilation. The lateral phoneme /l/ assimilates to the point of articulation of a following consonant in a way which is similar although not identical to the manner in which a nasal consonant assimilates to a following consonant. Spanish has no velar lateral, and labial laterals do not exist in any language. Given these two constraints, laterals assimilate to a following consonant in the same manner as do nasals.

[el̯ tio] el tio 'the uncle'
[el̯ niño] el nino 'the child'
[el̯ ĉiko] el chico 'the boy'
[el̃ lab̯ero] el llavero 'the keycase'

3.1.2.1 Evidence in favor of the definition of the feature [occlusive] presented in Section 1.2.4.2.1.1. The feature [occlusive] is defined in Section 1.2.4.2.1.1 in such a way that nasals and laterals are [+ occlusive] in spite of the fact that there is, in both cases, an alternate escape route for the air stream. Moreover, the feature [occlusive] is defined in such a way that the flaps and trills, [r] and [r̃], are not considered [+ occlusive] but [- occlusive] since the contact which is made in the articulation of these sounds is a secondary effect of narrowing the gap between the tip of the tongue and the gum ridge.

In support of the claim that this definition is correct, is the fact that the type of occlusion involved in the articulation of nasals and laterals is relevant to the proper understanding of the assimilation phenomena described here. For the occlusion involved in nasals and laterals is produced by direct muscular control of the position of the tongue. Since there is no phonemic contrast among nasals or among laterals in the context ___ C, the speaker effects the occlusion in the way which involves the least effort; namely, at the point of articulation of the following consonant. On the other hand, the main articulatory gesture involved in /r/ and /r̃/ is not an occlusion, but rather a narrowing of the gap between the tongue and the gum ridge. Since this narrowing is not an occlusion it is not subject to the assimilatory process which affects nasals and laterals.

Thus, defining occlusive as in Section 1.2.4.2.1.1 makes it possible to explain why nasals and laterals, but not vibrants, assimilate. In terms of feature economy, this definition of [occlusive] makes it possible to specify with just two features ([+ sonorant, + occlusive]) the class of segments which undergoes assimilation.

3.1.3 Formulation of a combined assimilation rule for nasals and laterals.

In the previous section, it was shown that nasal and lateral assimilation are closely related. In addition, the features [+ sonorant] and [+ occlusive] were shown to be sufficient to define the class of segments which assimilate.

Nevertheless, there is a difficulty involved in combining nasal and lateral assimilation into a single rule, because lateral assimilation applies in fewer contexts than does nasal assimilation. Rule (3.6) is an extension, to include laterals, of the earlier nasal assimilation Rule (3.4).

$$(3.6) \quad \begin{bmatrix} + \text{ sonorant} \\ + \text{ occlusive} \end{bmatrix} \longrightarrow [\alpha \text{ PA}] \, / \, \underline{\quad} \begin{bmatrix} + \text{ cns} \\ \alpha \text{ PA} \end{bmatrix}$$

However, Rule (3.6), if not restricted in some way, will produce feature complexes which do not correspond to existing segments. For example, the effect of applying Rule (3.6) to the word alba 'dawn' would be to convert the l to a segment marked [- high, - back, + anterior, - coronal, - dental], that is, a bilabial. Since, as indicated earlier, bilabial laterals do not exist, this application must somehow be blocked.

Harris (1969:20) discusses this difficulty, and in this instance, as well as in the difficulty which involves the term 'homorganic', suggests the general approach that the solution developed here in fact takes. His suggestion is that an assimilation rule such as Rule (3.6) be interpreted to apply within the limits of general restrictions for the segment types involved.

3.1.3.1 An extension of the linking use of Marking Conventions as a constraint on assimilation of laterals.

In Chapter Five, rules are presented which fill in the predictable features of various classes of laterals, for example, a rule specifies that all laterals in Spanish have one of the following points of articulation: dental, alveolar, palato-alveolar, or palatal. The rule has two parts, and is formulated as in Rule (3.7).

$$(3.7) \quad \text{(a)} \quad [+ \text{ lat}] \rightarrow [- \text{ back}]$$
$$\text{(b)} \quad [+ \text{ lat}] \rightarrow [+ \text{ cor}] \, / \, \begin{bmatrix} \phantom{+ \text{ ant}} \\ + \text{ ant} \end{bmatrix}$$

Rule (3.7a) stipulates that all laterals are [- back], and
Rule (3.7b) stipulates that a lateral cannot be [+ ant, - cor]
(i.e. bilabial).

In SPE (419ff.), rules such as (3.7) are called 'Marking
Conventions' and are deemed to be 'linked' to the other phonological rules in a way which permits the effects of certain
Marking Conventions to apply to the output of a phonological
rule. For example, if a new segment is introduced into a
word, the new segment, by virtue of 'linking', undergoes the
same Marking Conventions that apply to instances of that segment which occur in lexical matrices.

In order to account for the limitations on lateral assimilation,
I propose an extension of the concept of linking, which permits
the effect of absolute Marking Conventions[2] such as Rule (3.7)
to be interpreted as global constraints which apply at every
step of a derivation. This proposed extension of the concept
of linking operates as follows. 'Whenever an application of a
phonological rule would result in a feature configuration which
violates a provision of an absolute Marking Convention, then
that application is blocked.' Given this new 'linking' proposal,
and given Rule (3.7), Rule (3.6) is an accurate description of
nasal and lateral assimilation. It expresses the basic facts of
this phenomenon in a general way; and the limitations on lateral
assimilation are expressed by the same constraint which determines the possible points of articulation of laterals in general.

In this section, an analysis of nasal and lateral assimilation
has been proposed, and a rule has been formulated which
treats this assimilation as a unitary phenomenon. In addition,
various theoretical conclusions have been drawn from the data.

3.2 Lax stops and fricatives. Lax obstruent phonemes are
manifested as stops after pause, after nasals, and, for /d/ and
/y/, after /l/; they occur as fricatives elsewhere. The following sketch and accompanying examples illustrate this alternation
in detail.

Phoneme /b/:
[b] phonetic phrase initial: [bamos] <u>vamos</u> 'let's go'
    after nasal: [ambos] <u>ambos</u> 'both'
[b̷] all other environments: [ab̷soluto] <u>absoluto</u> 'absolute',
    [ezb̷elto] <u>esbelto</u> 'slender', [ab̷re] <u>abre</u> 'he opens',
    [arb̷ol] <u>arbol</u> 'tree', [ser b̷weno] <u>ser bueno</u> 'to be good',
    [aj b̷ino] <u>hay vino</u> 'there's wine'

Phoneme /d/:
[d] phonetic phrase initial: [damelo] <u>dámelo</u> 'give it to me'
    after nasal: [andar] <u>andar</u> 'to walk'
    after /l/: [aldea] <u>aldea</u> 'village'
[d̷] all other environments: [nad̷a] <u>nada</u> 'nothing',
    [nad̷je] <u>nadie</u> 'nobody', [aj d̷os] <u>hay dos</u> 'there's two',
    [loz d̷ias] <u>los dias</u> 'the days', [este d̷rama] <u>este drama</u>

'this play', [arde] <u>arde</u> 'it burns'

Phoneme /y/:
[y] phonetic phrase initial: [ŷa boj] <u>ya voy</u> 'I'm coming'
after nasal [uñ ŷate] <u>un yate</u> 'a yacht'
after /l/: [el ŷate] <u>el yate</u> 'the yacht'
[y] all other environments: [loz yates] <u>los yates</u> 'the
yachts', [mi yate] <u>mi yate</u> 'my yacht', [por yate] <u>por</u>
<u>yate</u> 'by yacht'

Phoneme /g/:
[g] phonetic phrase initial: [gandul] <u>gandul</u> 'loafer'
after nasal: [manga] <u>manga</u> 'sleeve'
[g̸] all other environments: [alg̸o] <u>algo</u> 'something',
[ag̸ronomia] <u>agronomía</u> 'agronomy', [erg̸o] <u>ergo</u> 'ergo',
[loz g̸algos] <u>los galgos</u> 'the greyhounds'

In conjunction with the formulation of a rule to describe this
alternation, five topics of a theoretical nature are discussed:
(1) why features are chosen as the basic unit of analysis rather
than segments (Section 3.2.1), (2) why rules which fill in blank
specifications are to be preferred over rules which change
pluses to minuses or vice versa (Section 3.2.2), (3) the need
for a formal equivalent of the term 'except' (Section 3.2.3.1),
(4) an additional use of the [α PA] notation (Section 3.2.3.2),
and (5) some additional support for the decision to label nasals
and laterals [+ occlusive] (Section 3.2.4).

**3.2.1 The use of features rather than segments as the
basic unit of analysis.** The environments for the stop and
fricative allophones of each of the four lax obstruent phonemes
could easily be described by writing a separate rule for each
phoneme. However, since the phonetic difference between the
two allophones is the same in each case (stop versus fricative)
and since the environments are virtually identical, the four
allophonic alternations should be analyzed as one phenomenon.
Therefore, the four rules should be combined into a single
rule. Examination of these four rules and of the possible ways
to combine them shows rather nicely why features, and not
segments, are the correct units in terms of which generalizations can best be expressed.
Consider first a rule for /b/ only.

$$(3.8) \quad \begin{bmatrix} - \text{son} \\ - \text{tns} \\ + \text{ant} \\ - \text{cor} \end{bmatrix} \longrightarrow \begin{Bmatrix} [+ \text{ocl}] \; / \begin{Bmatrix} || \\ [+ \text{nas}] \end{Bmatrix} \underline{\quad} \\ [- \text{ocl}] \; / \; \text{elsewhere} \end{Bmatrix} \begin{matrix} (a) \\ \\ (b) \end{matrix}$$

In Rule (3.8), the symbol $||$ indicates a phonetic phrase
boundary (see Harris 1969:23), and thus Rule (3.8a) specifies
/b/ as [+ occlusive] after pause or a nasal. Rule (3.8b) specifies /b/ as [- occlusive] in all other environments. The use of
the word elsewhere is not formal notation and is replaced in a
later version of the rule (see Rule (3.11).
The corresponding segment-oriented rule would read:

(3.8')   /b/ $\longrightarrow$ $\begin{cases} \text{[b] after pause, after nasal} & \text{(a)} \\ \text{[ƀ] elsewhere} & \text{(b)} \end{cases}$

If we now generalize the rule (ignoring the /l d/ and /l y/
sequences for the moment) to take in /d/, /y/, and /g/, the
feature-oriented rule is simplified whereas the segment-oriented
rule must be made more complex.

$$(3.9)\quad \begin{bmatrix} -\text{ son} \\ -\text{ tns} \end{bmatrix} \dashrightarrow \begin{cases} [+\text{ ocl}] \; / \; \begin{Bmatrix} || \\ [+\text{ nas}] \end{Bmatrix} \underline{\quad} & \text{(a)} \\[2em] [-\text{ ocl}] \; / \; \text{elsewhere} & \text{(b)} \end{cases}$$

$$(3.9')\quad \begin{bmatrix} /b/ \\ /d/ \\ /y/ \\ /g/ \end{bmatrix} \to \begin{cases} \begin{bmatrix} b \\ d \\ ŷ \\ g \end{bmatrix} \; / \text{ after pause or nasal} & \text{(a)} \\[3em] \begin{bmatrix} ƀ \\ đ \\ y \\ ǥ \end{bmatrix} \; / \text{ elsewhere} & \text{(b)} \end{cases}$$

Rule (3.9) is more general than Rule (3.8) and requires fewer
feature specifications than Rule (3.8). On the other hand, in
the case of the segment-oriented rules, the more general rule
requires the inclusion of more segments than the less general
rule. Thus, it can be seen that the feature presentation makes
possible the desired correlation between mechanically computed
economy (number of feature specifications) and generality of
description, whereas the segment-oriented presentation does not
make possible any similar correlation. Therefore, the selection
of features as the units for analysis is required in order to
yield a correct simplicity metric (see Section 2.7.1) and to allow
the framework to meet the level of explanatory adequacy (see
Section 0.4.3).
Furthermore, the feature complex which appears as input to
Rule (3.9) defines a 'natural class', a set of phonemes which
share certain phonetic properties. The class of segments subject to Rule (3.9) is the set of all and only the lax [- tense]
obstruents [- sonorant]. On the other hand, the list of phonemes in Rule (3.9') does not reveal the nature of the natural

class to which these phonemes belong. The list /b,d,y,g/ (which is a natural class) seems no more natural than the list /b,n,t,θ/ (which is not), when both are expressed as lists.

3.2.2 The distinctive features of lax obstruents. In the lexicon, each phoneme is represented by the smallest set of feature specifications which uniquely defines that phoneme. In some instances, alternative sets of specifications are equally economical, and, in these cases, the choice between the alternatives can be based upon grounds other than simplicity. Spanish obstruents can be classified in lexical entries as to manner of articulation either as shown in Figure 3.3 or as shown in Figure 3.4. The two classifications are equally economical.

Figure 3.3. Classification of manner of articulation of obstruents using [Ø occlusive] specifications for lax obstruents.

	p	t	ĉ	k	f	θ	s	x	b	d	y	g
[ocl]	+	+	+	+	-	-	-	-	Ø	Ø	Ø	Ø
[tns]	+	+	+	+	+	+	+	+	-	-	-	-

Figure 3.4. Classification of manner of articulation of obstruents using [Ø tense] specifications for tense fricatives.

	p	t	ĉ	k	f	θ	s	x	b	d	y	g
[ocl]	+	+	+	+	-	-	-	-	+	+	+	+
[tns]	+	+	+	+	Ø	Ø	Ø	Ø	-	-	-	-

The phonetic data presented in Section 3.2 suggests that the phonemes /b d y g/ should not be specified for the feature [occlusive] (i.e. that Figure 3.3 is correct), and that the rule which specifies the allophones of these phonemes replaces the [Ø occlusive] specifications with plus and minus specifications in the appropriate environments. However, a rule may also change a feature value from plus to minus or vice versa. Therefore, an alternative to the analysis just suggested would be to specify these phonemes in the lexicon as [- ocl] or as [+ ocl] (as shown in Figure 3.4), and then write a rule to change the value of the feature [ocl] in the appropriate environments. These two analyses are equally possible; however, they imply different assumptions concerning the basic structure of the Spanish consonant system.

The analysis sketched in Figure 3.3 assumes that the feature
[tense] differentiates lax obstruents from all others, whereas
the analysis sketched in Figure 3.4 assumes that the features
[tense] and [occlusive] are both distinctive in the matrices of
lax obstruents. In addition, the two analyses make different
assumptions as to the relationship between the occlusive allophones and the nonocclusive allophones.

Rule (3.9) is formulated so as to apply to phonemes which
are not marked for the feature [occlusive] specifying them as
either [+ occlusive] or [- occlusive]. Thus, both allophones
(of each phoneme) are accorded equal status. Neither allophone
is considered 'basic'. On the other hand, in Figure 3.4, the
lax obstruent phonemes are marked [+ occlusive]. This desig-
nation suggests that the occlusives are somehow more basic
than the fricatives, which are modified pronunciations. Thus,
an important factor in the choice between these two analyses
is a decision as to whether or not it is legitimate to consider
the stop allophones to be more basic than the fricative allophones.

Before attempting to decide this issue, it must be acknowl-
edged that these two possible analyses do not stand as equals
from a theoretical viewpoint. The analysis sketched in Figure
3.3 has an advantage in that it does not require that any feature specifications be changed from plus to minus. I assume,
as does Postal (1964:55ff.), that in the absence of other factors which have a bearing on the adequacy of the grammar as
a whole, an analysis which does not reverse feature specifications is superior to one which does reverse feature specifications.[3] The burden of proof is thus upon the advocate of
[+ occlusive] lax obstruent phonemes, and it is to that proof
that I now direct my attention.

As pointed out in Harris (1969:38), the pronunciation of lax
obstruents is subject to a certain degree of variation. Returning for a moment to the sketch of the data originally presented
in Section 3.2, a refinement must be made. Whenever a word
boundary precedes a lax obstruent, an occlusive pronunciation
is possible, depending upon considerations of speech style.
This means that hay vino 'there's wine' might be either [aj
bino] (if the words are separated) or [aj ƀino] (if they are
run together). On the other hand, the v of buen vino will
always be a stop. The possible pronunciations are [bwen bino]
(if the words are separated) and [bwem bino] (if they are run
together). To sum up, after word boundary, the occlusive
allophone occurs in all environments in a slow speech style,
and in some environments in a fast speech style, whereas the
fricative allophone occurs only in certain environments and in
those environments only in a fast speech style.

Allophonic distributions which follow this pattern have received a fairly consistent treatment in studies of variation. The
pronunciation which surfaces most frequently in the slower,
more monitored speech style is considered basic, and the other

allophone is treated as a modification of the basic pronunciation. This general practice seems correct to me, and thus I accept the [+ occlusive] allophones as basic and adopt, therefore, the analysis upon which Figure 3.4 is based.

3.2.3 Specifying the environment of the rule: Formal difficulties. If the analysis in terms of [+ occlusive] phonemes is to be accepted, then the rule which relates lax obstruent phonemes to their respective allophones must state that these phonemes are pronounced as nonocclusives in certain environments. However, the environments in which the [- occlusive] allophones occur are quite difficult to state succinctly, as pointed out by Harris (1969:40). As a first approximation, let us consider Rule (3.10), which is patterned after Harris' rule.

$$(3.10) \quad \begin{bmatrix} - \text{ son} \\ - \text{ tns} \end{bmatrix} \longrightarrow [- \text{ ocl}] \ / \ \begin{cases} [- \text{ son}] & \\ \begin{bmatrix} - \text{ nas} \\ - \text{ lat} \end{bmatrix} & \\ [- \alpha \text{ cor}] & \end{cases} \begin{bmatrix} \underline{\quad\quad} \\ \alpha \text{ cor} \end{bmatrix} \quad \begin{matrix} \text{(a)} \\ \\ \text{(b)} \\ \\ \text{(c)} \end{matrix}$$

Rule (3.10) states that a lax obstruent becomes [- occlusive] (a) after obstruents, (b) after vibrants and vowels, and (c) after any segment which does not agree with the obstruent as to the value of the feature [coronal].

Rule (3.10) yields the desired phonetic results, namely, stop and fricative allophones, each in their appropriate environments. The rule, however, is rather complex. For in order to express the environment for the fricative allophones, four feature specifications are required. Nevertheless, as Harris (1969:40) remarked, it is relatively easy to state the environment for the fricative allophones in informal terms. Lax obstruents 'appear as continuants except initially and after homorganic noncontinuant [+ occlusive]) sonorants'.

This informal statement of the environment of the fricatives suggests, in addition to a description of this alternation, its explanation. Apparently, what causes the stop allophone to occur after a nasal or lateral is the fact that an occlusion already exists when the speaker begins to form the obstruent. In order to incorporate this explanation into the rule, it is necessary to express in feature notation what Harris expresses by his words 'except after homorganic noncontinuant sonorants'. Thus, further motivation is provided for positing a formal equivalent for the term 'homorganic'. Rule (3.10) is reformulated in Section 3.2.3.2, using the [α PA] notation. But, first, a formal equivalent for the term 'except' must be introduced and incorporated into the rule.

3.2.3.1 The use of the alpha notation as a formal equivalent for 'except'. Harms (1968:71-73) proposes a use of the alpha (α) notation at the beginning of the environment part of a rule which makes it possible to eliminate the environment for the

fricatives from Rule (3.10) and to use instead the environment
of the stop allophones, which is easier to express. In Rule
(3.11), only the environment for the occlusives is given; the
use of the alpha both as the coefficient of the feature [occlu-
sive] and at the beginning of the environment specifies vacu-
ously that the lax obstruents are [+ occlusive] in the presence
of the stated environment and converts them to [- occlusive]
allophones in its absence.

$$
(3.11) \quad
\begin{bmatrix} -\text{ son} \\ -\text{ tns} \end{bmatrix}
\dashrightarrow [\alpha \text{ ocl}] \ / \ \alpha
\left\{
\begin{array}{l}
|| \\[4pt]
[+\text{ nas}] \\[4pt]
\begin{bmatrix} +\text{ lat} \\ \beta \text{ cor} \end{bmatrix}
\end{array}
\right\}
\begin{bmatrix} \underline{} \\ \beta \text{ cor} \end{bmatrix}
\quad
\begin{array}{l}
(a) \\[6pt]
(b) \\[6pt]
(c)
\end{array}
$$

3.2.3.2 An additional use of the [α PA] notation. Rule
(3.11) of necessity specifies the feature [coronal] in order to
handle instances of /l d/; that is: after a lateral, only a segment which agrees with the lateral as to the feature [coronal]
is [+ occlusive]. However, as in the case of nasal assimilation,
such a specification seems incorrect. For the relevant factor
is whether or not the lax obstruent is preceded by a homorganic sonorant occlusive. Thus, in order to state the rule in
a manner which is closer to Harris' informal statement, the
reference to the feature [coronal] should be replaced with the
[α PA] notation. Moreover, this replacement makes it possible
to collapse parts (b) and (c) of Rule (3.11). The result is
Rule (3.12).

$$
(3.12) \quad
\begin{bmatrix} -\text{ son} \\ -\text{ tns} \end{bmatrix}
\dashrightarrow [\alpha \text{ ocl}] \ / \ \alpha
\left\{
\begin{array}{l}
|| \\[4pt]
\begin{bmatrix} +\text{ ocl} \\ \beta \text{ PA} \end{bmatrix}
\end{array}
\right\}
\begin{bmatrix} \underline{} \\ \beta \text{ PA} \end{bmatrix}
$$

This rule is both simpler and descriptively more adequate than
the formulation given as Rule (3.11).
    As was suggested in Section 2.7.1, one of the major goals of
phonological theory is the establishment of a one-to-one relationship between mechanical simplicity and descriptive adequacy.
The claim presented here is that since Rule (3.12) is descriptively more adequate than Rule (3.11), the abbreviation which
makes Rule (3.12) possible is a valid device.

**3.2.4 Additional support for the definition of the feature
[occlusive] given in Section 1.2.4.2.1.1.** The behavior of the
lax obstruents lends some additional support to the decision to
label nasals and laterals as occlusives. What causes the stop
allophone of an obstruent to appear after a nasal or lateral is
the fact that an occlusion already exists when the speaker begins to form the obstruent. Thus, the definition of the feature

occlusive given in Section 1.2.4.2.1.1--namely, the presence of
occlusion at the main point of articulation regardless of whether
or not the air stream is stopped completely--makes it possible
to explain the behavior of lax obstruents, not merely describe
or state the environments for each of the allophones of these
lax obstruents.

3.3 **Obstruent voicing assimilation.** In most instances, an
obstruent assimilates to a following consonant with respect to
voicing. Perhaps the most noticeable instance of this phenomenon is the voicing of /s/ when followed by a voiced consonant: [mizmo] mismo 'same', [dezde] desde 'from'. However,
the rule is a very general one. A [- occlusive] obstruent
assimilates to any following consonant, and a [+ occlusive] obstruent assimilates to a following consonant other than a liquid.
Examples of this assimilation are [atmosfera] atmósfera 'atmosphere', [aφsoluto] absoluto 'absolute', [xuʐ̮gar] juzgar 'to
judge' [izla] isla 'island'. Examples of occlusives followed by
liquids which do not assimilate are [platikar] platicar 'to chat',
[premjo] premio 'prize', [trabaxo] trabajo 'work'.
When voicing assimilation takes place, only the feature
[voiced] changes; that is, the first segment assimilates in voicing to the voiced or voiceless second segment. The segment
which undergoes the rule retains its own value with respect to
the feature [tense]. For this reason, distinct symbols are
used for the voiced allophones of tense stops [p̬, t̬, k̬], and
for the lax stops [b, d, g].
The rule which accounts for this assimilation process is
written with an abbreviatory device known as angled parentheses (< >).[4] This device is used to abbreviate two rules,
one of which includes, in two or more segments, feature specifications not included in the other rule. The fullest version
of the rule is applied first, and the ordering is disjunctive
(see Harms 1968:66).
The two rules to be abbreviated are Rule (3.13) for instances
of /p, t, k/, and the more general Rule (3.14) for the remaining instances.

$$(3.13) \quad \begin{bmatrix} + \text{ cns} \\ - \text{ son} \\ + \text{ ocl} \end{bmatrix} \longrightarrow [\alpha \text{ voi}] \; / \; \underline{\quad} \left[\begin{array}{c} + \text{ cns} \\ \alpha \text{ voi} \\ \left\{ \begin{array}{c} [- \text{ son}] \\ [- \text{ nas}] \end{array} \right\} \end{array} \right]$$

$$(3.14) \quad \begin{bmatrix} + \text{ cns} \\ - \text{ son} \end{bmatrix} \longrightarrow [\alpha \text{ voi}] \; / \; \underline{\quad} \begin{bmatrix} + \text{ cns} \\ \alpha \text{ voi} \end{bmatrix}$$

The abbreviation of Rule (3.13) and Rule (3.14) is Rule
(3.15).

$$(3.15) \quad \begin{bmatrix} + \text{ cns} \\ - \text{ son} \\ <+ \text{ ocl}> \end{bmatrix} \longrightarrow [\alpha \text{ voi}] \ / \ \underline{\hspace{1cm}} \begin{bmatrix} + \text{ cns} \\ \alpha \text{ voi} \\ < \begin{Bmatrix} [- \text{ son}] \\ [+ \text{ nas}] \end{Bmatrix} > \end{bmatrix}$$

3.4 Lax vowels. In Section 1.2.3 a series of [- tense] vowel variants were described. These vowels are shortened, somewhat relaxed, and pronounced with less precision than the [+ tense] vowels. They occur in unstressed syllables in close proximity to a stressed vowel, e.g. [musɪka] <u>música</u> 'music'. The rule which describes this phenomenon is a variable rule (see Section 3.0.1). Whether it applies or not in any given situation depends not only on the linguistic context but also upon the degree of care being exercised at the moment by the speaker. Navarro (1968:44) states that 'the pronunciation of unaccented vowels depends especially upon the degree of care with which one speaks'.

Since, to date, the various linguistic and sociolinguistic factors which contribute to laxing have not been studied in detail, I am unable to present here a fully formulated variable rule which accounts for the hierarchy of factors involved. The main factor, however, does seem to be the location of the vowel in question with respect to the accented syllable of the word. Thus, a vowel is likely to be more relaxed if it is in a syllable adjacent to the syllable which receives the main stress. Therefore, I would suggest as a first approximation Rule (3.16), an optional rule.

$$(3.16) \quad V \dashrightarrow [- \text{ tns}] \ // \ C_0 \ [+ \text{ str}]$$

In Rule (3.16) the double slash indicates a mirror-image rule; that is, the rule is an abbreviation of Rule (3.17).

$$(3.17) \quad V \dashrightarrow [- \text{ tns}] \ / \ \begin{Bmatrix} \underline{\hspace{1cm}} \ C_0 \ [+ \text{ str}] \\ [+ \text{ str}] \ C_0 \ \underline{\hspace{1cm}} \end{Bmatrix}$$

The term C_0 is shorthand for 'zero or more consonants' (see SPE:62). The rule optionally allows the laxing of a vowel which occurs in the syllable adjacent to the syllable of the stressed vowel.

3.5 Glides. In this section, the phonemic status of various types of glides and the rules which account for them are discussed. Since the analysis of Spanish glides has been the subject of some controversy, some discussion of previous treatments is presented in conjunction with the analysis set forth here. Briefly, my claim regarding Spanish glides is that there are two types of glide and a separate rule introduces each type.

One of these rules is an Everywhere Rule which accounts for
most high glides within words; the other is a Variable Rule
which serves primarily to account for glides derived from
[- high] vowels and glide formation at word boundary.

3.5.1 The phonemic representation of glides. The controversy concerning Spanish glides has focused upon the correct
phonemic representation of these sounds. Should they be
represented phonemically as vowels, as consonants, or as
glides?

3.5.1.1 The traditional analysis. The traditional analysis
of Spanish glides was to assign them to the vowel phonemes
/i/ and /u/ (see, e.g. Trager 1939, King 1952, Chavarría-
Aguilar 1951, Silva-Fuenzalida 1953). This viewpoint is also
reflected in the Spanish orthography, which represents glides
as i and u in most cases. To my mind this traditional analysis
(or more exactly, a reinterpretation of the traditional analysis
in terms of an Everywhere Rule) is, in large measure, correct.
But before demonstrating that this is so, the other points of
view should first be examined.

3.5.1.2 Bowen and Stockwell versus Saporta. In Bowen and
Stockwell (1955 and 1956) and in Saporta (1956), two opposing
points of view are set forth. The former authors take issue
with the traditional analysis and suggest that the [j] and [w]
should be represented as /y/ and /w/, respectively. Thus,
for example, the [j] of [bjen] bien 'good' and the [y] of [mayo]
mayo 'May' are considered allophones of the phoneme /y/.
In contrast, Saporta (1956) makes the claim that the Bowen
and Stockwell analysis is not possible due to the occurrence of
minimal pairs such as [abjerto] abierto 'open' versus [abyekto]
abyecto 'abject' and [desjerto] desierto 'desert' versus [dezyelo]
deshielo 'I unfreeze'. Bowen and Stockwell, in turn, respond
that these pairs are not really minimal, and that the second
word in each pair has an internal 'open juncture' (+) which occurs immediately before the [y], e.g. [dez+yelo] /des+yelo/
deshielo versus [desjerto] /desyerto/ desierto.
Although Bowen and Stockwell's positing of open juncture in
these words is questionable, it is interesting to note that there
is a morpheme boundary everywhere that Bowen and Stockwell
posit 'open juncture'. This is a good illustration of the fact
that phonology and morphology are closely related, and not
autonomous as claimed by some phonemicists.

3.5.1.3 Alarcos and Harris. As Alarcos (1968:153ff.) and
Harris (1969:26) pointed out, the difficulties encountered by
the analysts discussed in the previous section are due, in
large part, to their failure to recognize that a given phone
need not be represented by the same phoneme everywhere it
occurs. Both Alarcos and Harris analyze some instances of [j]

as /i/ and others as /y/. Harris (1969:28), for example,
represents <u>son hienas</u> 'they are hyenas' as /son#ienas/ --->
[sónjénas] <u>and</u> <u>son yemas</u> 'they are egg yolks' as /son#yemas/
--->[soñjemas]. (I have substituted my symbols for Harris'
in these representations.) In addition, it should be noted that
Harris (1969) deals with Mexican Spanish, and in Mexican Spanish, the initial segments of <u>hienas</u> and <u>yemas</u> are pronounced
as glides in colloquial speech. Throughout this section, I
speak of phonemes as 'representations of' sounds (e.g. /i/ is
a representation of [j]; or conversely, [j] is represented by
/i/). The reader who is familiar with American structuralist
descriptions may be accustomed to hearing them phrase this in
the reverse order.

3.5.1.4 Two phonemic representations for Spanish glides.
As shown in Section 3.5.1.3, it is not necessary to assume that
all phonetic glides are represented by the same phoneme. In
fact, there are good reasons to assume that Spanish has two
types of glides derived from different sources. In Sections
3.5.1.4.1 and 3.5.1.4.2, I present an analysis which derives
some glides from glide phonemes, and which derives other
glides from vowel phonemes.[5] There are two important differences between these two types of glides. First, only in the
case of the glides derived from vowel phonemes is there variation between [+ syllabic] and [- syllabic] pronunciations, e.g.
[mi amor] versus [mjamor] for <u>mi amor</u> 'my love'. Second,
vowel phonemes do not undergo the spirantization rule discussed in Section 3.6. (See Harris 1976 for discussion of
these two points.)

3.5.1.4.1 Glide phonemes. In Figure (3.1), I have included
two glide phonemes /j/ and /w/ in the inventory of Spanish
phonemes. As I explained in Section 3.0, this is because the
distinction between a glide and a high vowel must in some
cases be specified in the lexicon.

3.5.1.4.1.1 Harris' argument in favor of glide phonemes.
That it is necessary to represent some phonetic glides as
glides at the phonemic level was pointed out by Harris (1969:
31, 122-123). He cites two sorts of data to support this con-
tention.
(1) Verbs such as <u>cambiar</u> 'to change' are conjugated with
stem-final glides ([kámbjo], etc.) whereas verbs such as
<u>ampliar</u> 'to amplify' are conjugated with stem-final stressed
vowels ([amplío], etc.). Both classes of verbs are quite large.
Moreover, to my knowledge, no viable solution has been offered
as an alternative to Harris' proposal that verbs of the <u>cambiar</u>
type be represented with a stem-final /j/ at the systematic phonemic level.
(2) Words such as <u>áureo</u> 'golden', <u>náufrago</u> 'shipwreck',
<u>láudano</u> 'laudanum', <u>ventrílocuo</u> 'ventriloquist' show stress on

the fourth from the last orthographic vowel. If the u's in
these words are represented as phonemic vowels, stress must
be placed on the fourth phonemic vowel from the end of the
word, a pattern which otherwise does not exist in Spanish.

Harris points out that it is theoretically possible to account
for words like áureo by positing a rule of Glide Formation which
would be ordered before the Stress Assignment Rule. Harris
rejects this solution, however, for the following reason: pairs
such as [pais] país 'country' versus [pajsano] paisano 'country-
man' and [baul] baul 'suitcase' versus [bawlero] baulero 'porter'
show that Spanish must have a Guide Formation Rule which depends upon stress placement. For the root in each pair should
be represented by a vowel, since this segment surfaces as a
vowel in the first member of each pair. After Stress Assignment, the high vowel in the second member of each pair is converted to a glide, since it is not stressed. The Glide Formation Rule which effects these conversions must therefore follow
the Stress Assignment Rule. Harris (1969:31) argues that it
would be unlikely for a language to have 'two nearly identical
rules that cannot be collapsed'. They cannot be collapsed because one is ordered before Stress Assignment and the other
is ordered after Stress Assignment. Furthermore, words like
país and baul would be incorrectly reduced to *[pajs] and
*[bawl] if there were a Glide Formation Rule ordered before
Stress Assignment. Harris, therefore, concludes that only the
second rule, the one which follows Stress Assignment, exists
and that words like áureo 'golden' should be represented with
glides at the systematic phonemic level.

**3.5.1.4.1.2 The representation of glide phonemes in the
lexicon.** Harris' reasoning is, in my opinion, correct insofar
as it applies to what Chomsky and Halle (1968:380-389) call
'systematic phonemic matrices'. However, it is not necessary
to represent any segment explicitly as a glide in the lexicon.

The representations of morphemes which are listed in the
lexicon are related to the systematic phonemic matrices by a
special set of rules called 'Everywhere Rules' which are discussed more fully in Chapter Five. Everywhere Rules are expressed in the same notation used by Chomsky and Halle in
their Marking Conventions (SPE:400ff.). This 'markedness'
notation consists of two values for features: u (unmarked)
and m (marked). One of the Everywhere Rules which I propose for Spanish can be used to avoid representing any segment explicitly as a glide in the lexicon. Most nonconsonantal
segments can be entered in the lexicon without any specification
as to whether they are [+ syllabic] (vowels) or [- syllabic]
(glides). In markedness notation, these segments are given
as [u syllabic], which means 'unmarked' or 'unspecified' for
the feature [syllabic].

The rule rejected by Harris can then be reformulated as an
Everywhere Rule which specifies that a high nonconsonantal

segment which is contiguous to a vowel is specified as a glide
[- syllabic]. Thus the u of áureo is marked [u syllabic] in
the lexicon, and the Everywhere Rule specifies this segment as
[- syllabic] at the systematic phonemic level. The systematic
phonemic level of áureo, therefore, is /awreo/, just as suggested by Harris. On the other hand, the high nonconsonantal
segments /i/ and /u/ of país and baul, respectively, which are
vowels, must be marked as exceptions to this Everywhere Rule.
In markedness notation, they are [m syllabic], 'marked'
[syllabic].

Essentially, I am asserting that the analysis which Harris
originally formulated, but rejected, is correct; there are two
Glide Formation Rules, one ordered before Stress Assignment
and the other ordered after Stress Assignment. These two
rules are formulated in Section 3.5.2. But first it is necessary to show that to postulate two Glide Formation rules is a
reasonable analysis. In order to motivate the inclusion of two
rules which are so similar, it is necessary to show that there
are important differences between them. This Section
(3.5.1.4.1) has dealt with glide phonemes specified by the
Everywhere Rule; Section 3.5.1.4.2 discusses glides which are
derived from vowel phonemes and then explains the differences
between these two types of glides.

3.5.1.4.2 Phonetic glides derived from vowel phonemes. The
glides discussed in Section 3.5.1.4.1 are glide phonemes. Other
phonetic glides are specified at the systematic phonemic level as
vowels and are converted to glides by a Low Level Allophonic
Process Rule. Phonetic glides which are derived from vowel
phonemes differ from glide phonemes in that, in the case of
the vowel phonemes, there are variant pronunciations (the
vowel phonemes are sometimes pronounced as vowels, sometimes
as glides), whereas the glide phonemes are always pronounced
as glides.

The Everywhere Rule discussed in Section 3.5.1.4.2 applies obligatorily to any sequence of nonconsonantal segments,
one of which is high, and specifies the high nonconsonantal
segment as a glide, unless the high nonconsonantal segment
has been explicitly marked as an exception, i.e. marked
[m syllabic]. Application of this rule to a given word yields
the same result every time the word occurs in an utterance;
bien 'good' is always [bjen], with a glide, and país 'country'
is always [pais], with a vowel. There is no variation of glide
and vowel in these words based upon speed, style, or degree
of monitoring. Pronunciations such as *[bien] for bien and
*[pajs] for país do not exist.

There are, however, other sequences of nonconsonantal segments which are pronounced sometimes with glides and sometimes with vowels. For example, teatro 'theatre' can be pronounced [teatro] or [tĕatro]; the e can be either [+ syllabic]
or [- syllabic]. Most instances of variant pronunciations fall

into one of the following categories: (1) neither vowel is high,
as in teatro, or (2) the sequence of vowels is formed as a result of two words coming together; e.g. mi amor 'my love',
which can be pronounced [miamor] or [mjamor].

In addition, some sequences which involve a high vowel
followed by another vowel within a word are subject to variation. In this last category, there is considerable difference
of opinion among speakers regarding which segments are subject to glide versus vowel variation, and which are not. For
example, some speakers accept [raðio] as a variant of [raðjo]
radio 'radio'; and others do not. For any given speaker, only
glides which are not in variation with vowels are formed by the
Everywhere Rule. All other glides are derived from vowel phonemes by the Variable Rule.

In Figure 3.5, variant pronunciations of several examples are
listed. For each word, the first pronunciation given is the one
which exhibits the highest degree of monitoring. In this pronunciation, all nonconsonantal segments are pronounced as
vowels. In the second pronunciation listed for each example,
a vowel is replaced by a glide. In addition to these two pronunciations, there are two other pronunciations of some of the
examples. An unstressed vowel can be relaxed (see Section
3.4) and a mid vowel can be converted to a mid glide rather
than a high glide (see Section 1.2.3.2). Altogether, there are
four pronunciations of poeta 'poet': [poeta] with a full normal
(albeit unstressed) o, [pɔeta] with a laxed o, [pɔ̯eta] with a
mid glide, and [pweta] with a high glide. This range of possibilities can best be accounted for by a Variable Rule. Moreover, it is easy to identify linguistic and sociological factors
that determine which pronunciation of one of these examples is
most likely to be used in a given situation; for example, a glide
is more likely in fast informal speech. Clearly, therefore,
glides such as those which occur in the second pronunciations
of the examples listed in Figure 3.5 should be accounted for by
a Variable Rule which takes into account the socioeconomic and
geographical background of the speaker, speed of speech, position of stress, presence of boundaries, and possibly other factors as well. Furthermore, this variable rule is capable of
applying to strings of words. The Everywhere Rule, on the

Figure 3.5. Glides derived from nonhigh vowels.

teatro 'theatre'	[te-a-tro], [tja-tro]
poeta 'poet'	[po-e-ta], [pwe̯-ta]
toalla 'towel'	[to-a-la], [twa-la]
mi amor 'my love'	[mi-a-mor], [mja-mor]
tu edad 'your age'	[tu-e-ðað], [twe-ðað]
te adoro 'I adore you'	[te-a-ðo-ro], [tja-ðo-ro]

other hand, cannot apply to strings of words and must be obligatory. Because of these differences, the two rules cannot be combined. These differences then prove that it is reasonable to postulate two Glide Formation Rules in spite of the fact that both rules specify nonconsonantal segments as glides.

3.5.2 Glide Formation Rules

3.5.2.1 An Everywhere Rule.
The rule which specifies that a high nonconsonantal segment is a glide if adjacent to another vowel, is an Everywhere Rule and is formulated as shown in Rule (3.18).

$$(3.18) \quad \begin{bmatrix} u\ syl \\ -\ cns \end{bmatrix} \dashrightarrow \left\{ \begin{array}{ll} [-\ syl]\ //\ \begin{bmatrix} \overline{+\ high} \end{bmatrix}\ V & \text{(a)} \\[2em] [+\ syl] & \text{(b)} \end{array} \right.$$

Part (a) of Rule (3.18) specifies that the unmarked, or most natural value of the feature [syllabic] is minus in the case of a high nonconsonantal segment which is adjacent to a vowel. Part (b) of Rule (3.18) specifies that for all other nonconsonantal segments, the unmarked value is plus. The glides of words such as [awreo] aureo 'golden' are [u syllabic] in the lexicon and Rule (3.18) specifies that they are [- syllabic]. Words such as baul which are pronounced with a high vowel in contact with another vowel (i.e. [baúl], not *[báwl]), are represented in the lexicon with a high vowel which is marked [m syllabic]. According to conventions which govern the operation of rules such as (3.18) (see Section 5.3), these [m syl] specifications are converted to [+ syl] specifications, and Rule (3.18) therefore yields the correct phonetic realizations of these words as well.

3.5.2.2 A Variable Rule.
Rule (3.19) is a tentative formulation of a variable rule to account for instances of glide formation not specified by the Everywhere Rule discussed in Section 3.5.2.1.

$$(3.19) \quad \begin{bmatrix} +\ syl \\ -\ stress \end{bmatrix} \dashrightarrow [-\ syl]\ //\ \left\langle \begin{array}{c} [+\ high] \\ \begin{bmatrix} -\ high \\ -\ low \end{bmatrix} \\ [+\ low] \end{array} \right\rangle\ \left\langle \begin{array}{c} \begin{Bmatrix} \emptyset \\ + \end{Bmatrix} \\ \# \end{array} \right\rangle\ [+\ syl]$$

The material inside the large angled parentheses specifies those properties of the environment which are relevant to the likelihood of operation of the rule. The first part of the environment states that the higher the vowel, the greater the likelihood that the rule will apply. The second part indicates that the rule is most likely to apply when there is no boundary or morpheme boundary between the two segments, and less likely to apply when the two segments are separated by a word boundary. Since the phonetic phrase boundary ($\|$) is not mentioned, application of the rule is blocked whenever the phonetic phrase boundary ($\|$) is present between two vowels. Material not enclosed within large angled parentheses are obligatory conditions for application of the rule. Thus the rule only applies to an unstressed vowel which is in contact with another vowel.

3.6 Spirantization of glides.

As pointed out in Section 1.2.4.1.1, when the glide [w] occurs in word-initial position, or after a vowel, it is frequently converted to the obstruent [ǥ^w]. The same conversion applies to the glide [j]; the result is the obstruent [y]. An example of the [j]-[y] alternation can be seen in the ending for third person preterite of second and third conjugation verbs, namely, /-ieron/. This ending begins with [j] when the verb stem ends in a consonant [saljeron] salieron 'they left', and begins with [y] when the verb stem ends in a vowel [kreyeron] creyeron 'they believed'.

A better way to view the contexts involved in this alternation is in terms of syllable structure. Glides are converted to the spirants [y] and [ǥ^w] when they are syllable-initial, and not otherwise. This is expressed in Rule (3.20).

$$(3.20) \quad \begin{bmatrix} - \text{ cns} \\ - \text{ syl} \end{bmatrix} \rightarrow \begin{bmatrix} + \text{ cns} \\ - \text{ son} \end{bmatrix} / - \underline{\quad}$$

Rule (3.20) must be ordered before Rule (3.12) which specifies that lax obstruents are occlusives after pause or after a homorganic nasal or lateral. This ordering accounts for the pronunciation of the initial segments of words like huevo in phrases such as [u gʷeβo] un huevo 'an egg'.

Since the glides which are produced by the Variable Glide Formation Rule do not undergo Spirantization (Rule (3.20)), Spirantization must be ordered before Glide Formation.

3.7 Conclusion.

This chapter has dealt with a number of phenomena which are generally recognized as being allophonic in nature. That is, rules have been proposed which relate a set of abstract segments (phonemes) to a set of concrete manifestations (allophones).

In Chapter Four, another set of rules which are somewhat more abstract in nature is discussed. These rules typically change more features of the segments involved, they apply only within word boundary, they are not subject to variation, and they are not productive. For these reasons, they are less widely accepted as valid rules of phonology than those treated here in Chapter Three.

NOTES

1. The most efficient matrix is the one which contains as few 'plus' and 'minus' specifications as possible. In Chapter Five, the 'plus', 'minus', and 'zero' (blank) specifications are replaced by 'marked' and 'unmarked' specifications.

2. In Chapter Five of this book, rules of this type are called 'Everywhere Rules', and a distinction is drawn between absolute Everywhere Rules and those which express different degrees of naturalness. The linking convention proposed here applies only to the absolute Everywhere Rules.

3. I refer to Postal's (1968:53ff.) naturalness condition, which he calls a 'weaker version of the invariance condition'. The invariance condition is defined by Chomsky (1964:91ff.) as follows: 'Each phoneme P has associated with it a certain set of "defining features" and...wherever P occurs in a phonemic representation, there is an associated occurrence of [the set of defining features] in the corresponding phonetic representation.' That is, the invariance condition allows rules which fill in 'zero' specifications, but does not allow rules which change 'plus' specifications to 'minus' or vice versa. Postal's weaker version of this condition allows rules which change feature specifications, but associates a higher cost with them than with rules which do not violate invariance. Thus, all other things being equal, an analysis which satisfies the invariance condition is to be preferred to one which violates it.

4. Harris (1969:42) provides a formulation of Voicing Assimilation which does not require the use of angled parentheses. However, his version of the rule is based upon specifications of /p,t,k/ as [+ voiced], and these specifications have been rejected here (see Section 1.2.5.7), so his version of the rule cannot be used.

In passing, I should like to point out what I take to be an oversight in the formulation of Harris (1969:44) Rules 53 and 54. It appears that these rules yield incorrect results. At the point in a derivation when Harris' Rule 54 applies, the segments [p,t,k] are specified as [+ voiced]. Therefore Harris' rule will copy this [+ voiced] specification onto an [s] in a word like este. This produces the incorrect output *[ezte].

5. In Chapter Four, another source of Spanish glides is discussed. Some Spanish mid vowels diphthongize under stress, thus producing [we] and [je] sequences. In terms of the classification discussed in this chapter, the glides introduced by the Diphthongization Rule group with the glides derived from glide phonemes.

CHAPTER 4

WORD-LEVEL PHONOLOGY

4.0 Introduction. The Word-level Phonology Rules, which are discussed in this chapter, differ from the Low-level Allophonic Process Rules discussed in Chapter Three, in that the Word-level Phonology Rules are characterized by the following properties. (1) Unlike Low-level Allophonic Process Rules, the Word-level Phonology Rules change several features of the segments to which they apply. Some of them, in fact, introduce new segments into a word, delete segments from a word, or substitute one segment in place of another. (2) Whereas the Low-level Allophonic Process Rules are not affected by the presence of word boundaries, the Word-level Phonology Rules, as the name implies, apply only within a word. (3) The Word-level Phonology Rules are not subject to variation. (4) The Word-level Phonology Rules are ordered closer to the morphological component than are the Low-level Allophonic Process Rules. (5) With the exception of Epenthesis, and, to some extent, Stress Assignment, the Word-level Phonology Rules are not productive, i.e. they do not apply to new words which are coined or borrowed from other languages.

In contrast to the Low-level Allophonic Process Rules, there is considerable disagreement among linguists concerning the validity of the Word-level Phonology Rules, and concerning their status as phonological rules.

4.1 Linguistic units and boundaries which affect the application of phonological rules. The rules presented in Chapter Three apply within a phonetic phrase regardless of the presence of word boundaries within the phrase. However, if a phonetic phrase boundary (| |) intervenes between two segments of the required context, application of a Low-level Allophonic Process is blocked. In addition to the phonetic phrase, there are other linguistic units which are pertinent to the application of phonological rules. These other units and the effects of their boundaries are discussed in Sections 4.1.1 through 4.1.4.

4.1.1 The syllable. A syllable is a basic unit of pronunciation--a sequence of segments which is pronounced together as a unit. A syllable consists of a vowel nucleus which sometimes is preceded and/or followed by glides and/or consonants. The syllable serves as the 'domain' of some phonological rules; that is, some rules apply to a segment only if it is syllable-initial or syllable-final. For example, Spirantization of Glides (see Section 3.6) applies only to segments which are syllable-initial. In addition, syllable structure is pertinent to the Lowering of High and Mid Vowels (see Section 1.2.2.3.1) and to Stress Assignment (see Section 4.3.1.1). For a discussion of other effects of syllable structure, see Hooper (1972).

4.1.2 The morpheme. A morpheme is a basic unit of form--a sequence of segments which has a recognizable and consistent relationship with some linguistic entity which is distinct from the string itself. It is not clear whether or not any bona fide phonological rules apply over the domain of a morpheme in Spanish. In Harris (1969), a number of rules are formulated using a morpheme boundary as part of the required context. For example, a rule is given which deletes the theme vowel of a verb (e.g. /abl + a + r/ hablar 'to speak'), when the theme vowel is followed by a non-tense vowel, as in [aβlo] hablo 'I speak'. The rule is formulated as in (4.1).

$$(4.1) \quad V \longrightarrow \emptyset \ / \ + \ \underline{\quad} \ + \begin{bmatrix} V \\ - \text{ tense} \end{bmatrix}$$

Although (4.1) makes reference to the morpheme boundaries which precede and follow the vowel to be deleted, this seems to be simply a convenient way to limit the application of the rule to theme vowels. It does not seem to be the case that a vowel is deleted because it is the only segment in a morpheme. In other words, it does not seem that the morpheme, as a type of unit, is pertinent to the application of the rule. It seems, rather, that the pertinent aspect of the vowels which are deleted is the fact that they are theme vowels. On the other hand, in the case of the Spirantization of Glides, it does seem reasonable to claim that the glides are converted to spirants because they are in syllable-initial position.

4.1.3 The root. A root is the basic, most significant morpheme of a word. In /abl + a + mos/ hablamos 'we speak', /abl/ is the root, and /a/ and /mos/ are grammatical morphemes. There are rules which apply over the domain of a root. For example, when a vibrant is root-initial, it is always /r̃/. The rule which states this fact, Tensing of Initial r (see Section 5.6.3), cannot be formulated in terms of syllables or morphemes, because there are syllable-initial and morpheme-initial instances of lax /r/. For example, the /r/ of /abl + a + ron/ hablaron 'they spoke' is both morpheme-initial and syllable-initial. Nor is it possible to formulate the Tensing of Initial r rule over the domain of a word. A vibrant which is root-initial is always /r̃/, whether or not it is word-initial. When a prefix is applied to a root which begins with a vibrant (e.g. /r̃ei/ rey 'king'), the resultant word also contains the tense root-initial vibrant: /bir̃ei/ virrey 'viceroy'. If the pertinent domain of Tensing of Initial r were the word, we would expect some root-initial instances of lax /r/. However, there are none.

4.1.4 The word. A word is not as easy to define as the linguistic units discussed in Sections 4.1.1 through 4.4.3. However, for the purposes of the present discussion, it is possible to consider that a word boundary occurs wherever there is a space in standard orthography.[1] There are rules which apply within the domain of a word, for example, Epenthesis. When the phonemic representation of a word begins with /s [+ consonantal]/, an [e] is added before the /s/: escuela 'school', estacion 'station', escribir 'to write'. There are no exceptions. The rule which expresses this fact is formulated as in (4.2).

(4.2) $\emptyset \longrightarrow e \ / \ \# \ \underline{\quad} \ s \ [+ \ consonantal]$

That the domain of Rule (4.2) is neither the root nor the morpheme, is shown by instances of prefixing such as /in + skribir/ inscribir 'to inscribe' and /tran + skribir/ transcribir 'to transcribe'. These words have root-initial and morpheme-initial /sk/, and the words are realized as [inskriƀir, transkriƀir], not [* ineskriƀir, *traneskriƀir]. Hooper (1972) presents an analysis of Epenthesis which is based upon syllable structure. However, the Epenthesis Rule itself is best formulated in terms of the word, since only word-initial /s [+ consonantal]/ sequences undergo the rule.

Epenthesis is an example of a rule which requires the presence of a word boundary at the beginning of the context for application. The word boundary does not intervene between elements of the context, and thus Epenthesis is a Word-level Phonology Rule as defined in Section 4.0. Although the other rules discussed in this chapter do not require the presence of a word boundary, they all share the property that word boundary is never permitted to intervene between segments specified in their environments.

4.2 The problem of abstractness. As pointed out in Chapter Two, generative phonology differs from the earlier taxonomic view of phonemics in that generative phonology is more abstract. This added abstractness has been the subject of considerable controversy among generative phonologists and, as

pointed out in Section 3.2.2, a number of attempts have been
made to constrain phonological analyses so as to preserve a
close relationship between phonetic representations and phonemic representations, and thus decrease the abstractness of
phonemic representations. In general, a less abstract phonological analysis is likely to be accepted by more linguists than
a more abstract analysis.

4.2.1 Factors which contribute to abstractness. Abstractness is not a technical term, but rather as it is used here an
impressionistic one. Therefore, it is not possible to arrive at
a mechanical measurement of the degree of abstractness of a
particular analysis. However, it is possible to stipulate what
properties of an analysis are generally considered to contribute
to its abstractness. The following factors all contribute to the
abstractness of a phonological analysis: differences between
phonetic and phonemic representations (Section 4.2.1.1), neutralization (Section 4.2.1.2), the use of boundaries (Section
4.2.1.3), and the use of nonphonetic features (Section 4.2.1.4).

**4.2.1.1 Great differences between phonetic representations
and proposed underlying forms.** As mentioned in Section
3.2.2, Postal (1964:55ff.) has shown that the underlying form
of a morpheme does not contain feature specifications which are
at odds with the phonetic shape of that morpheme, unless there
is a good reason to posit those specifications. Unless there is
a good reason to do otherwise, one always posits underlying
forms which do not require rules which change the values of
features. For this reason, when a proposed systematic phonemic representation differs greatly from the phonetic representation of that form, the proposed systematic phonemic representation is considered abstract. For example, a proposed underlying form /kok + e + o/ for [kweθo] cuezo 'I cook' requires the
application of at least three rules, one which deletes a segment
(the theme vowel /e/ is deleted), another which radically modi-
fies a segment (/k/ ---> [θ]), and a third which replaces a
single segment with a diphthong (/o/ ---> [we]). Therefore,
this proposed underlying form is considered quite abstract and
the validity of the analysis is questioned. Presumably, the reason for doubts concerning the validity of analyses of this sort
lies in the assumption that a native speaker is unlikely to memor-
ize a word in terms of a representation which differs so greatly
from its phonetic shape.

4.2.1.2 Neutralization. When two occurrences of the same
sound (e.g. [θ]) are represented as two different phonemes
(e.g. as /θ/ in /θero/ cero 'zero' and as /k/ in /medik + ina/
medicina 'medicine'), this fact contributes to the abstractness of
the analysis. The abstractness is further increased, in this
case, by the fact that there are other instances of /k/, which
occur in an environment identical to the environment of /k/ in

medicina, and which are realized as [k] (e.g. [kilo] /kilo/ kilo
'kilogram').

4.2.1.3 The use of boundaries in phonological rules. When
a boundary symbol (especially '+', the morpheme boundary) is
included as a part of the environment of a rule, in order to
limit the application of the rule to certain cases, this inclusion
contributes to the abstractness of the rule (see the example
discussed in Section 4.1.2).

**4.2.1.4 The use of nonphonetic features in phonological
rules.** As explained in Section 3.2.2, there is a close relationship between the phonetic structure and the phonological behavior of segments. Usually, segments which undergo a particular rule share certain phonetic properties, and these phonetic properties are used to stipulate which segments undergo
the rule and which do not. In the case of each of the rules
formulated in Chapter Three, it was possible to specify, using
phonetic features, the class of segments to which the rule applies. Occasionally, it is not possible to specify the class of
segments to which a rule applies using only phonetic features.
In these cases, a nonphonetic feature is posited in order to
distinguish segments which undergo the rule from those who
do not. For example, in Section 4.3.1.5, a special feature
[diph] is used to distinguish mid vowels which diphthongize
when stressed (poder 'to be able' versus puedo 'I can') from
those which do not (comer 'to eat' versus como 'I eat). The
use of nonphonetic features always contributes to the abstractness of the analysis.
   Nonphonetic features are of various types. (1) Abstract
phonological features are features which define phonological
behavior of segments, but do not refer to phonetic properties,
e.g. [diph]. (2) Abstract morphological features refer to
properties of entire morphemes, e.g. [1 conjugation] [+ mascu-
line]. (3) Syntactic features, such as [+ verb], [+ noun], are
used in phonology when a rule applies in one way to members
of a particular syntactic category and in another way to other
forms. For example, Spanish Stress Assignment applies in one
way to verbs and in another way to all other forms. The use
of any of these types of features contributes to the abstractness of the analysis.

4.2.2 Evaluation of abstract analyses. It is not possible
to arrive at a mechanical measurement of the abstractness of
a particular analysis. Nor is it possible to compare mechanically the disadvantages of abstractness with the advantages of
the greater generality which this abstractness makes possible.
In other words, it is not possible mechanically to decide
whether abstractness, in a particular analysis, has an overall
positive effect on the analysis or an overall negative effect on
it. Nevertheless, evaluations of this sort are frequently needed

in order to decide which of two analyses of the same data is preferable. In Sections 4.3 through 4.9, a number of Word-level Phonology Rules are discussed in relation to the problem of abstractness. In conjunction with the valuation of these rules, the following theoretical issues are discussed. (1) What is the relationship between synchronic and diachronic linguistics? (2) What types of justification can be presented in support of an abstract rule? (3) How should a phenomenon which is partially but not fully predictable be treated in a formal grammar? (4) What are the basic units in terms of which the phenomena of Word-level Phonology should be analyzed?

4.3 A set of interrelated Word-level Phonology Rules. In the remaining sections in this chapter, a number of rules which are related to each other in various ways are discussed. These rules have all been dealt with in previous studies (see references given in Section 4.4). They are the following: Stress Assignment (in lexical categories other than verbs), Velar Softening, Palatalization, Final -e̲ Deletion, Diphthongization, and Lenition.

4.3.1 A brief statement of the rules. In the sections which follow, each of the rules to be discussed in this chapter is stated and explained briefly. Each rule is discussed further in later sections devoted to the evaluation of rules of this sort.

4.3.1.1 Stress Assignment in lexical categories other than verbs. In Rule (4.3), the symbol $C_\emptyset$ signifies 'zero or more consonants', $\breve{V}$ stands for a vowel which is [- strong], and - represents syllable boundary. The parentheses enclose optional elements.

$$(4.3) \quad V \longrightarrow [+ \text{ stress}] \ / \ \underline{\quad} \ (C_\emptyset(\breve{V} -)C_\emptyset \ V)C_\emptyset \ \#]_{[- \text{ verb}]}$$

The rules abbreviated by this notation are disjunctively ordered, which means that the fullest expansion is applied first, and if the complete environment specified in the rule is matched by the shape of the word, then the antepenultimate vowel is stressed; otherwise the penultimate vowel is stressed if there are two or more vowels; if the word contains only one vowel, it is stressed.

4.3.1.2 Velar Softening. The formulation given in (4.4) expresses the surface facts of Velar Softening.

$$(4.4) \quad \begin{Bmatrix} k \\ g \end{Bmatrix} \longrightarrow \begin{Bmatrix} \theta \\ x \end{Bmatrix} \ / \ \underline{\quad} \ \begin{bmatrix} - \text{ cns} \\ - \text{ back} \end{bmatrix}$$

The velar stops /k/ and /g/ are softened to the fricatives [θ] and [x], respectively, when followed by a front vowel.

Pairs such as [mediko] médico 'doctor' versus [mediθina]
medicina 'medicine' and [elektriko] eléctrico 'electric' versus
[elektriθidad] electricidad 'electricity' illustrate this alternation
and also show that the analysis under discussion is essentially
reflected in the standard orthography. The letter c is pronounced [k] before [a,o,u] and [θ] before [e,i].

4.3.1.3 Palatalization. The following pairs illustrate another
alternation involving velars, which has been called Palatalization.

[aksial] axial 'axial' versus [exe] eje 'axle'
[řefleksiƀo] reflexivo 'reflexive' versus [řeflexo] reflejo
  'reflection'
[laktiko] láctico 'lactic' versus [leĉe] leche 'milk'
[nokturno] nocturno 'nocturnal' versus [noĉe] noche 'night'

This alternation is described in Rule (4.5). The feature
[native] effects an abstract subdivision of the lexicon into two
categories. Words marked [+ native] are those words which
underwent the normal sound change processes as Vulgar Latin
developed into Modern Spanish. Words marked [- native] are
those which have been borrowed from Classical Latin in more
recent times, and which thus failed to undergo some or all of
the sound changes.

$$(4.5) \quad \begin{Bmatrix} ks \\ kt \end{Bmatrix} \quad \dashrightarrow \quad \begin{Bmatrix} x \\ ĉ \end{Bmatrix} \quad / \quad \left[\underline{\hspace{1cm}} \atop + \text{ native} \right]$$

4.3.1.4 Final -e Deletion. In Foley (1965) and in Harris
(1969), words which have plural forms ending in /es/ are
represented at the phonemic level with a final /e/. This /e/
is then deleted from the appropriate singular forms after the
rule of Plural Formation applies. In general, a final /e/ is
deleted if it is preceded by [y] or by a single voiced coronal
consonant (ley/leyes, rey/reyes, merced/mercedes, ataud/
ataudes, estación/estaciones, papel/papeles). After a /θ/ or
/s/, the /e/ is deleted from some words (luz/luces, bus/buses),
and retained in others (roce/roces, base/bases). After other
consonants and after clusters, the /e/ is retained (combate,
confite, leche, plebe, poste, eje, conde). In Harris (1969:179)
it is shown that it is possible to group words like luz and bus
with the papel, estación group, by assuming that the coronal
consonants [θ] and [s] are voiced at the point in the derivation
at which the Final -e Deletion Rule applies. Therefore, the
Final -e Deletion Rule can be written so that it deletes final /e/
after a single voiced coronal consonant, after a vowel, or after
y. A preliminary formulation of this rule is given as Rule
(4.6).

$$(4.6) \quad e \longrightarrow \emptyset \ / \ V \left\{ \begin{array}{c} \begin{bmatrix} + \text{cor} \\ + \text{voi} \end{bmatrix}_{\emptyset}^{1} \\ y \end{array} \right\} \ \underline{\hphantom{xx}} \ \#$$

4.3.1.5 Diphthongization. Unstressed [e] and [o] alternate with the stressed diphthongs [wé] and [jé], respectively, in some words (pensar/pienso, beneficio/bien, poder/puedo, bondad/bueno) but not in others (temer/temo, comer/como). Traditionally, verbs such as pensar and poder which undergo this change have been classified as 'stem changing verbs'. However, it is not a characteristic of the stems /pod/ and /pens/ that determines these alternations, but rather a special characteristic of the vowels themselves. That is, it is the vocalic segment, and not the lexical entry as a whole, which is marked with a special feature to indicate that it diphthongizes when stressed. In Rule (4.7) a description of this phenomenon is given. The symbols E and O are used to refer to mid vowels which are marked to undergo this rule.

$$(4.7) \quad \left\{ \begin{array}{c} \acute{E} \\ \acute{O} \end{array} \right\} \longrightarrow \left\{ \begin{array}{c} je \\ we \end{array} \right\} \ / \ \left[\underline{\hphantom{xxxx}} \atop + \text{native} \right]$$

4.3.1.6 Lenition. In native words, tense intervocalic stops are converted to lax stops. For example, [nataθjón] natación 'swimming' is presumed to be [- native] and thus retains its intervocalic [t]. On the other hand, [nadar] nadar /natar/ 'to swim' is presumed to be [+ native]. Therefore, the underlying /t/ is converted to a [d]. The Lenition Rule is tentatively formulated as Rule (4.8).

$$(4.8) \quad \begin{bmatrix} + \text{ocl} \\ + \text{native} \end{bmatrix} \longrightarrow [- \text{tense}] \ / \ V \ \underline{\hphantom{xx}} \ V$$

4.3.2 Relationships among the rules. Each of the rules discussed in Section 4.3.1 is quite abstract; and therefore, the validity of each rule, considered in isolation, is subject to question. In this chapter it is claimed that what makes rules such as those sketched in Section 4.3.1 viable as parts of a theory of phonological competence, is the ways in which they are related to each other and the logic and order of the overall system which results from the inclusion of the set of those particular rules in the grammar. Thus, when a relationship between two rules is established, both rules are strengthened. However, a claim that a relationship exists between two or more rules must itself be carefully examined before it is accepted as support for the existence of the rules.

The following relationships between the rules of Section (4.3.1) have been claimed in previous studies (see, in

particular, Foley 1965 and Harris 1969). (1) Final -e Deletion
is said to simplify the analysis of Stress Assignment and Velar
Softening (Section 4.4.2). (2) It is claimed that Velar Softening and Palatalization are related in that a common step is included in both processes (Section 4.8). (3) Velar Softening is
claimed to include Lenition as a step (Section 4.8). (4) Stress
Assignment and Diphthongization are claimed to depend upon a
common abstract feature (Section 4.6.4.3). I do not accept all
of these relationships as valid. Some of the relationships,
nevertheless, are valid, and these relationships do lend some
support to the validity of the entire set of rules.

**4.4 The relationship between synchronic and diachronic lin-
guistics.** This section takes up the relationship between the
rules of Section 4.3 and historical sound change rules.

4.4.1 Sound changes and rules of phonology. As mentioned
earlier, all of the rules of Section 4.3 are relfexes of well-
known historical processes. See, for example, the following
descriptions: for Stress Assignment, Elcock (1960:10ff., 39ff.);
for Velar Softening, Lapesa (1959:57), Boyd-Bowman (1954:
22,32); for Palatalization, Lapesa (1959:91), Boyd-Bowman (1954:
40ff., 137ff.), Spaulding (1962:36, 96-97); for Final -e Deletion,
Boyd-Bowman (1954:55ff.), Spaulding (1962:87); for Diphthongization, Menéndez Pidal (1950:110ff., 144ff.), Lapesa (1959:92),
Boyd-Bowman (1954:48ff., 93ff.), Spaulding (1962:82), Alarcos
(1968:215ff.); for Lenition, Menéndez Pidal (1950:240ff.), Lapesa
(1959:58), Boyd-Bowman (1954:30-31), Spaulding (1962:92-93).

The first incorporation of these rules into a synchronic grammar occurs in Foley (1965). Stress Assignment is discussed in
Foley's Section 5.3, Velar Softening in Section 2.7, Palatalization in Section 1.6, Final -e Deletion in Section 3.2, and Lenition in Section 1.8. They are also all discussed in Harris
(1969).

**4.4.2 The relationship between sound changes and syn-
chronic rules.** Given these correspondences between proposed
synchronic rules and known historical processes, the question
arises as to the relationship between synchronic and diachronic
grammar. The question is interesting from two perspectives:
(1) that of the speaker (Section 4.4.2.1), and (2) that of the
analyst (Section 4.4.2.2).

4.4.2.1 From the perspective of the speaker. Looking first
at the speaker, we might ask the following: as the surface
forms of lexical items change as a result of historical processes,
to what degree do these changes produce modified lexical entries, and to what degree do the historical changes become synchronic rules to be learned by future generations of speakers?

Consider, for example, the Latin past participle ending -tus.
For the most part, this suffix has yielded modern Spanish -do
(hablado, vivido, etc.). However, in the case of certain verbs,

the t of tus was not in intervocalic position, and therefore did not undergo Lenition (vuelto, suelto, muerto, etc.). In some cases, the combination of the /t/ of the participial ending with the stem-final consonant of the verb produced still other re- sults, for example, the combination /kt/ produced [č] by Pala- talization (/dik + to/ --- [dičo]). The diachronic description of the above data is relatively clear. However, there are at least two possible synchronic analyses. (1) The underlying past participle ending is /do/, and in the case of certain verbs, special participles must be learned. (2) The underly- ing past participle ending is /to/, and the Palatalization and Lenition Rules yield the phonetic results in dicho, hecho, on the one hand, and hablado, vivido, on the other.

Both statements represent claims concerning the question as to what happens when the surface forms of words change due to sound changes. Analysis (1) suggests that the irregular participles were relexified after the historical changes took place. Analysis (2), on the other hand, represents the hy- pothesis that the underlying forms have remained more or less constant and that reflexes of the historical changes are incor- porated into the competence of speakers who live long after the productive period of the historical changes themselves.

Both theories are completely compatible with what little direct evidence exists concerning the nature of human mental pro- cesses. Ideally, it would be empirical evidence that would determine which of these two theories is to be preferred. Un- fortunately, at the present time there is no more evidence for one than for the other.

4.4.2.2 From the perspective of the linguist. From the standpoint of the analyst, the central issue is the validity of using historical data as evidence for or against a synchronic rule. In my opinion, the fact, by itself, of the existence of an historical process does not constitute evidence in favor of a corresponding synchronic rule. Typically, speakers of a language have no idea of the history of that language and, consequently, are not capable of using historical data as a basis for the formulation of underlying forms. In attempting to provide evidence in favor of a particular underlying form, the linguist must point to data which is available to contempo- rary speakers. Frequently, words which are related deriva- tionally to a particular form are considered relevant to the underlying representation of that form. For example, the existence of nocturno can be said to provide evidence for an underlying form /nokte/ for noche.

Returning to the example involving participles, one might suggest that /dik + to/ is a valid underlying form for dicho, because it is possible to derive both digo and dice from the same root /dik/ with reference to other phonological rules (Lenition in the case of digo and Velar Softening in the case of dice). This analysis does parallel the historical development of these forms. However, since historical evidence is not to be accepted as evidence in favor of a proposed analysis, one must look elsewhere for support for the underlying representation of the root /dik/. There are related forms (dictado, dictum) which contain the sequence [dik] phonetically as well as phonemically. These forms exist in contemporary Spanish, and are therefore available to contemporary speakers. It is logically possible, therefore, to suggest that speakers construct underlying /dik/ for the verb decir even though the /k/ never surfaces as [k] in a verb form. The claim being made here is only that this analysis is logically possible and that the cognates provide some evidence in favor of the underlying form of the verb. The analysis is not to be taken as proven. The semantic relationships between decir and dictado and dictum are not entirely clear, and the rules which produce the surface verb forms are rather abstract. Only if /dik/ is shown to be viable on the basis of additional synchronic data, can it be considered an appropriate underlying form for decir. We might therefore answer the earlier question concerning the use of historical data by saying that, for the linguist, the history can frequently suggest directions in which to search for plausible analyses, but when it comes to evaluation of a possible analysis, history is of no use.

4.5 The concept of independent motivation. Since historical accuracy is not to be accepted as a proof of an abstract analysis, other types of synchronic evidence (in addition to the examination of related forms) are needed. Two additional types of argument are frequently cited: (1) that the abstract underlying forms themselves are justified, and (2) that the rules which yield the correct results are justified. In each case, the claim is made that a form or a rule is justified because it is useful in the analysis of a number of otherwise unrelated phenomena. This constitutes the claim that the underlying form or the rule in question is 'independently motivated'.

4.5.1 Independent motivation of a rule. In the previous section, two possible analyses of past participles were sketched: one involving underlying /to/ endings and one involving underlying /do/ endings. The advantage of underlying /to/ endings is that it facilitates explanation of the irregular forms such as suelto, muerto, dicho, etc. However, since the surface manifestation of regular participles includes a [do] ending, the analysis which posits underlying /to/ is the more abstract analysis, and some justification is required. In support of this analysis, the claim can be made that the rule which is required to convert /to/ to [do] in the regular forms, would be required in a grammar of Spanish even if the irregular participles did not exist. The rule in question is the Lenition Rule described in Section 4.3.1.6. It is proposed as a rule of Spanish primarily in order to account for consonant alternations between native and learned words such as natación/nadar, recipiente/recibir, descripción/describir. The stems of the first word in each pair, nat-, recip-, and descrip- must be related at some level of analysis to the stems of the verbs nad-, recib-, describ-, and it makes sense to claim that these sets of forms are related in that the stem-final segment of the first word of each set fails to undergo Lenition (either because the V___V environment is not met or because the word is marked [- native]), whereas the second word in each pair does undergo this rule.

If this analysis is correct, then the Lenition Rule must be included in a grammar of Spanish, and it can be used in the explanation of the surface form of regular participles without any additional cost. In other words, the existence of pairs like natación/nadar provides motivation for the Lenition Rule which is independent of the analysis of regular and irregular past participles.

Although there are differences of opinion concerning the force of arguments of this type and concerning the applicability of this argument to specific cases, there seems to be general agreement that a theoretical construct is more plausible (all other things being equal) if it participates in the explanation of a number of otherwise unrelated phenomena than if it has been created solely to deal with one problem.

4.5.2 Independent motivation of an underlying form. The preceding section illustrates independent motivation of a rule. It is also the case that a nonobvious underlying form can be said to be more strongly motivated if it facilitates the analysis of more than one phenomenon.

Both Foley (1965) and Harris (1969) represent words which form plurals ending in -es (flores, voces, papeles, etc.) with stem-final /e/ at the systematic phonemic level. This /e/ is then deleted by the Final -e Deletion Rule (Section 4.3.1.2) from singular forms in which it does not appear. An argument in favor of these abstract underlying representations has been made by Harris (1969:177) based upon the claim that these representations (with stem-final /e/ which sometimes fails to surface in singular forms) make easier the analysis of three distinct phenomena which are unrelated to each other. The three rules which are simplified by stem-final /e/ are the following: Plural Formation (Section 4.5.2.1), Stress Assignment (Section 4.5.2.2), and Velar Softening (Section 4.5.2.3).

4.5.2.1 Plural Formation. On the surface, the plural forms of nouns and adjectives differ from the singular in one of the following ways: (1) some plural forms show suffix -es (papel/ papeles), (2) others show the suffix -s (conde/condes), (3) and a third class do not show contrasting singular versus plural forms (el lunes/los lunes). Saporta (1959) suggests three allomorphs for the plural morpheme, namely, (-∅, /es/, and /-s/). However, given a rule which reduces a sequence of two identical segments to one instance of that segment, and given abstract stem-final /e/ as posited by Foley and Harris, the plural morpheme can be expressed as the single form /s/. Word-final /e/ is then deleted in the contexts specified in Section 4.3.1.4, that is, it is deleted from the appropriate singular forms, but not from plurals.

4.5.2.2 Stress Assignment. Positing the final /e/ entirely eliminates word-final stress in nouns and adjectives and makes it possible to write the Stress Assignment Rule as a conditioned selection between penultimate and antepenultimate stress, thereby simplifying the Stress Assignment Rule. (This rule is discussed further in Section 4.6.)

4.5.2.3 Velar Softening. On the surface, Velar Softening applies before e and i (medicina versus médico) and at the end of words (voz versus vocal). Given the stem-final /e/ posited by Foley and Harris, the Velar Softening which occurs at the end of a word can be explained (as opposed to merely described or specified). Velar Softening applies to words such as voz because at the time of its application, the velar is followed by an e. The derivation of voz is as follows: /boke/ (Velar Softening) ----➤ [boθe], (Final-e Deletion) ---➤ [boθ]. The rejection of nonphonetic stem-final /e/ would require the complication of the Velar Softening Rule by the addition of the word-final environment ('__ #') as an additional environment where the rule would apply. This would 'describe' but would not really explain why word-final velars are softened.

4.5.2.4 Conclusion. If the stem final /e/ were posited merely in order to simplify the analysis of one phenomenon, the resultant analysis would not be a very convincing one. However, since the positing of stem-final /e/ simplifies three rules, it is argued that the psychological validity of this abstract segment is considerably greater.

4.6 Stress Assignment and the phenomenon of partial predictability. In this section, various treatments of Spanish stress are discussed.

4.6.1 Traditional description of Spanish stress. In the preparation of the Spanish orthography, the académicos of the Real Academia Española (1885) realized that Spanish stress is at least partially predictable, i.e. words ending in vowels, n, or s tend to be stressed on the next to last syllable (zapato, combate, examen, lunes) and words ending in other consonants tend to be stressed on the last syllable (arroz, papel, merced, virtud). On the other hand, they also realized that this prediction does not work for all cases, so they provided a way of marking stress in cases which violate their basic rules. A written accent mark is used in standard orthography whenever

the stress does not conform to the two patterns just specified,
e.g. lápiz, amén, papá, múltiple. This procedure is, in intent
and in essence, the equivalent of the phonologists' postulation
of general rules and the use of special features to specify exceptions to those rules.

4.6.2 The American structuralist treatment of Spanish stress.
American structuralists generally did not accept analyses which
required the specification of exceptions. The Academy's rule is
not universal, and since the structuralists, given conditions
such as bi-uniqueness, could not see a way to construct a rule
which would work for all cases, they therefore considered stress
to be unpredictable, and marked it as phonemic. This resulted
in the counterintuitive marking of stress across the board, even
in completely regular cases of penultimate stress such as problema, palo, hablo, examen, etc.

4.6.3 Generative treatment of Spanish stress. There have
been a number of treatments of Spanish stress in the context
of generative phonology. The analysis described here is basi-
cally the treatment of Foley (1965) and Harris (1969). The
analysis is based partially upon the prediction of Spanish stress
with reference to certain aspects of syllable structure and partially upon the indirect marking of stress using a nonphonetic
feature.

4.6.3.1 Stress patterns in surface forms. In surface phonetic forms, stress occurs on the following syllables: (1) final
syllable: papel, arroz, salud; (2) penultimate: árbol, malo,
machete, problema, redondo; (3) antepenultimate: número,
ópera, símbolo; (4) fourth from the end: dándoselo, quítenmelo.

4.6.3.2 Elimination of final stress in underlying forms. As
pointed out earlier, final stress is eliminated from consideration
(in treatment of nouns and adjectives) by positing an underlying stem-final /e/ on words such as papel, arroz, and salud.
The resultant phonemic representations have penultimate stress:
/papele/, /aroθe/, /salude/. (Note that the postulation of this
/e/ also shifts certain words such as árbol /arbole/ from the
penultimate group to the antepenultimate group.)

**4.6.3.3 Elimination of stress four syllables from the end of
underlying forms.** Stress four syllables from the end occurs
only in compound forms such as dándoselo, in which the following constituent structure can be assumed: #dando#se#lo# (#
indicates word boundary). The stress does fall on the penultimate syllable of the verb, and the other two syllables are
clitic pronouns which are incapable of being stressed. Other
than in compounds of this type, stress never occurs four (or
more) syllables from the end of the word. As Harris (1969:
119) points out, words such as *tápadaga do not exist.

4.6.3.4 Penultimate versus antepenultimate stress. Given the elimination from underlying forms of these two patterns (final stress and stress four syllables from the end of a word), it is necessary only to specify whether a noun or adjective has penultimate or antepenultimate stress. The situation is further simplified, as Harris (1969:119) notes, by the fact that there are no words such as *tánampo with antepenultimate stress and a penultimate syllable which is closed by a consonant. Therefore, the choice between penultimate and antepenultimate stress is at least partially conditioned by the phonetic environment.

Consider now, pairs such as sábana 'sheet' versus sabana 'plain'. There is no physical difference between these two words besides the stress; they constitute the classical case of a 'minimal pair'. Some mark is required in the lexicon to distinguish between the two words.

4.6.3.4.1 Why stress cannot be marked directly in the lexicon. When commenting on Postal's naturalness condition, I suggested that in the absence of reasons to the contrary, two forms should ideally be differentiated one from the other by some physical feature rather than by an abstract feature. So, in this case, it might be suggested that the best procedure would be to mark the first a of sábana [m stress] in the lexicon, and formulate a general rule of stress assignment to specify penultimate stress for all words in which no segment is explicitly marked for stress in the lexicon. Given the abstract final /e/'s posited by Foley and Harris, this analysis would be equivalent to the use of the accent mark in standard orthography.

However, there is a problem. As pointed out in Harris (1974b), stress is defined in terms of the position of a syllable in a word, but the lexicon is a list of morphemes. The lexical entry which underlies número 'number' can surface with stress on any of the three syllables, or on none of them, depending on the structure of the entire word into which the morpheme /numer/ is inserted: número, numérico, numeroso, enumeración. It is therefore not possible to mark stress in the lexicon.

4.6.3.4.2 An abstract feature for the analysis of stress. Since the feature which effects the differentiation between penultimate and antepenultimate stress cannot be a physical feature, it must be an abstract diacritic. Although vowels cannot be marked either [+ stress] or [- stress] in the lexicon, a vowel can be marked as to whether or not it is capable of being stressed when it occurs in a penultimate open syllable.

I shall provisionally call the needed feature [S/P] ('stressed if penultimate'). Vowels which are stressed in open penultimate syllables are [+ S/P]; vowels which are unstressed in open

penultimate syllables are [- S/P]; vowels which occur in closed
penultimate syllables or never occur in a penultimate syllable
are not specified with regard to this feature.

Most attempts to account for stress placement within the
generative framework have been based upon a feature which
has the effect of [S/P]. However, there have been disagreements concerning the nature of this feature (phonetic or abstract?), its name ([tense], [long], [D], [X], and [strong]
are a few names which have been proposed), and its relationship to other rules which apply to vowels (particularly the
Diphthongization Rule).

4.6.3.4.3 The nature of the feature involved in Stress
Assignment. A brief review of former treatments of this feature will serve to illustrate some of the problems involved in
the analysis of Spanish stress. In his doctoral dissertation,
Foley (1965) called this feature [long]. Foley's feature pur-
ports to be a phonetic feature and figures in the analysis of
Diphthongization as well as Stress Assignment. [+ long] is
equivalent to [+ S/P] and [- long] vowels are subject to
Diphthongization. After the application of these two rules,
the distinction between [+ long] and [- long] vowels is erased
by a neutralization rule. Note, in passing, that Foley's analysis and the name he chose for the feature are reminiscent of
the diachronic situation regarding these vowels: for the most
part, it is accurate to relate the historically long vowels of
Latin to the [+ S/P] vowels of contemporary Spanish and to
relate the historically short vowels to Diphthongization.

In Harris (1969), a similar analysis of both phenomena is presented; Harris, however, replaces Foley's phonetic feature with
a diacritic [D] ([+ D] equals [- long]).[2] The feature in question must be a diacritic as suggested by Harris, and not a phonetic feature as proposed by Foley because there is no phonetic
difference between a vowel which is [+ S/P] and one which is
[- S/P]. The name, [D], while it has no phonetic content,
does refer to the phonological behavior of segments which are
so marked: [+ D] vowels are those which are subject to the
Diphthongization Rule, provided the other conditions of that
rule are met.

4.6.3.4.4 Stress Assignment and Diphthongization. As seen
in the previous section, Harris (1969) attempts to maintain the
relationship between Stress Assignment and Diphthongization.
In line with the earlier discussion concerning independent motivation, the psychological validity of the feature [D] is considered higher if this feature figures in the analysis of more
than one phenomenon. Harris (1969:119) recognizes that there
are words which constitute a problem for this relationship.
Venezuela, abuelo, consuelo (the noun), and a number of
others, constitute a paradox with regard to the feature [D].
They must all be derived from underlying forms containing a

[+ D] /o/ because of cognates such as venezolano, abolengo, consolar. However, in order for Stress Assignment to apply to these forms correctly, the penultimate vowel (the /o/) in each case must be [- D] ([+ S/P]). Because of paradoxical situations of this type, Harris concludes in a later paper (Harris 1974b) that Spanish has lost the relationship between Stress Assignment and Diphthongization and that two distinct diacritics are needed, one for Diphthongization (which he thereafter calls [+ diph]), and another for Stress Assignment. In accepting Harris' conclusion regarding these two diacritic features, I have opted to use the name [+ strong] for the diacritic feature which is relevant to Stress Assignment ([+ strong] equals [+ S/P]). This name, like [+ diph] says something about the phonological behavior of the segments thus marked. Specifically, it is plausible to claim that a penultimate syllable is stressed in Spanish if it is strong. A syllable can be strong either by virtue of its ending (a closed syllable is a strong syllable) or by virtue of the vowel itself (a syllable which contains a strong vowel is a strong syllable).

4.6.4 Conclusions. In this discussion of stress in lexical categories other than verbs, the following conclusions have been reached.

(1) Stress is largely predictable in Spanish. In some cases, a vowel must be marked as not stressable in an open penultimate syllable.

(2) A nonphonetic feature must be postulated in order to effect the lexical marking stipulated in conclusion (1).

(3) This nonphonetic feature cannot be equated with the nonphonetic feature which accounts for diphthongization.

4.7 Diphthongization. Traditionally, verbs such as poder/puedo were called 'radical changing verbs' and classified as irregular verbs along with other types of irregular verbs such as those which gain a hard consonant in certain forms (tener/tengo, conocer/conozco). However, there is an important difference between these two classes of verb. Whereas the hard consonant which is added to the conocer type verb is an idiosyncratic property of a set of lexical entries for verbs, the diphthongization phenomenon is not limited to verbs (bondad/bueno, beneficio/bien). Moreover, the diphthongization phenomenon is a property of a specific vowel segment, not a property of a whole root or stem. Because of this difference, the Diphthongization Rule is a phonological rule, whereas the rule which specifies the addition of hard consonants to the stems of certain verbs is not. Just as in the case of Stress Assignment, there is no phonetic difference between mid vowels which diphthongize and those which do not; the o's of comer and poder are identical. Therefore, as suggested earlier, a diacritic must be used to specify the application of the Diphthongization Rule.

Although the diacritic [+ diph] which is used to specify those
mid mowels which undergo Diphthongization is not, as believed
formerly, independently motivated by virtue of playing a role
in Stress Assignment, both the diacritic and the rule are nonetheless necessary elements for the analysis of Spanish. In
formulating the Diphthongization Rule one must consider its
relationship to two other rules (1) Glide Formation (Section
4.7.1) and (2) Spirantization (Section 4.7.2).

4.7.1 Diphthongization and Glide Formation. Diphthongization, as seen in Section 4.6, cannot be formally related to
Stress Assignment. Another point of controversy regarding
Diphthongization is the question of the relationship which may
exist between Diphthongization and Glide Formation. It is
possible to claim, as does the formulation given in Section
4.3.1.5, that the rule of Diphthongization converts a vowel
directly into a glide + e sequence, without intervening steps
in the derivation. However, given the existence of Glide Formation as an independent process, it is possible to claim that
Diphthongization, per se, merely creates ue and ie sequences
which are, in turn, converted to [we] and [je] by a Glide Formation Rule.

Harris (1976) takes the position that Glide Formation is not
a part of the diphthongization process, because Glide Formation
is a Variable Rule, and the glides which result from application
of Diphthongization do not occur in variation with vowels.
However, as pointed out in Section 3.5, there are two Glide
Formation Rules in Spanish, the Variable Rule and an Everywhere Rule. In my view, the best treatment of diphthongization does involve two steps: (1) the Diphthongization Rule
itself converts /o/ to [ue] and /e/ to [ie]; and (2) the Glide
Formation Everywhere Rule converts the high vowels thus produced into glides.

4.7.2 Diphthongization and Spirantization. If the glide
which results from application of the Diphthongization Rule is
in syllable-initial position, it will be converted to an obstruent
by the rule discussed in Section 3.6. As pointed out in that
section, the spirantization rule does not apply to all glides.
The variable glide formation rule must be ordered after ob-
struentization so that its output will not be subject to obstruen-
tization. The difference in the derivations of yerba 'herb,
grass' and hiena 'hyena' can now be stated as in Figure 4.1.

**4.8 Velar Softening, Palatalization, and the basic units of
analysis.** Throughout this study, it has been assumed that the
feature is the basic unit of phonological analysis. From a theoretical standpoint, the use of features as the basic unit implies
that linguistic competence can best be characterized in terms of
the individual properties which features represent. From a
practical standpoint, this implies that rules are to be formulated

Figure 4.1. Derivations of yerba 'herb, grass' and hiena 'hyena'.

Underlying forms:	/e rba/	/i ena/
	[+D]	[m syl]
Stress Assignment:	é	é
Diphthongization:	ié	–
Glide Formation Everywhere		
Rule:	j	–
Obstruentization:	y	–
Variable Glide Formation		
Rule:		j
	[yérba]	[jéna]

in terms of features. To take a specific rule, for example, Glide Formation, it can be assumed that a speaker knows one fact--that high vowels become glides, not two facts--that /u/ becomes [w] and /i/ becomes [j].

However, a closer examination of the rules under consideration in this chapter reveals an important distinction: some rules appear to be segment-oriented rather than feature-oriented.

4.8.1 **Feature-oriented versus segment-oriented rules.** Some of the rules discussed in this chapter seem to be quite similar to the Low-level Allophonic Process Rules discussed in Chapter Three, in that they involve changes which are most easily defined in terms of a change in one feature specification. Lenition is an example of this type of rule; the tense stops all become lax in the specified environment. Lenition is thus a feature-oriented rule. In other cases, however, it is not clear that the feature is the important unit. For example, Velar Softening and Palatalization involve changes which differ from the feature-oriented rules in two important ways: (1) the input and output segments differ from each other as to the specification of several features, not just one, and (2) the various segments which are subject to each rule do not all change in the same manner: /k/ becomes anterior [θ] when it is softened, but /g/ remains a velar [x]. For these two reasons, it seems correct to view these changes as the replacement of one segment by another, rather than as changes in individual features. I shall refer to these rules as segment-oriented rules.

This is not to say that it is impossible to formulate analyses of Velar Softening and Palatalization in terms of rules which change individual features. In fact, Harris (1969:162-177) presents feature-oriented rules for both phenomena. Harris' analyses are discussed in the next section.

4.8.2 **Feature-oriented analyses of Velar Softening and Palatalization.** In his analysis of Velar Softening, Harris

(1969:164)[3] proposes to decompose the process into the following steps.

1	2	3	4	5

$$k \longrightarrow t^s \longrightarrow d^z \longrightarrow z \longrightarrow s$$

$$g \longrightarrow \widip: J \longrightarrow \check{z} \longrightarrow \check{s} \longrightarrow x$$

The steps can be identified as follows: 1 Fronting, 2 Lenition, 3 Loss of the stop element, 4 Devoicing, and 5 Conversion of [š] to [x].

Harris also proposes breaking down the process of palatalization into the following steps.

1'	2'	3' (=5)

$$ks \longrightarrow y\check{s} \longrightarrow \check{s} \longrightarrow x$$

$$kt \longrightarrow y\check{c} \longrightarrow \check{c}$$

These steps can be identified as: 1' Palatalization, 2' Loss of y before palatals, and 3' equals 5.

In his analysis of these two phenomena, Harris specifies these steps as rules which are expressed in terms of features. In this manner, he is making two explanatory statements which are not evident in the surface presentation of the data which was given in Sections 4.3.1.2 and 4.3.1.3. First, process 1' can be seen as a mutual assimilation of two segments: [k] is fronted (palatalized) due to the attraction of the anterior segments [t] and [s], and these segments are raised due to the attraction of the [+ high] [k]. Second, each phenomenon is seen to apply uniformly to all inputs up to a point. That is, the component steps of Palatalization apply identically to [kt] and [ks] and the steps of Velar Softening apply identically to [k] and [g] with the exception, in both cases, of the final step 3'=5, which arbitrarily converts [š] to [x]. By positing this one arbitrary rule, Harris has reduced what at first seems to be two puzzles: (1) why does Velar Softening not apply identically to all segments? and (2) why does Palatalization not apply identically to all segments? to one puzzle (why does [s] become [x]?).

4.8.3 **Motivation for the feature-oriented analyses.** In terms of the concept of independent motivation, two comments are relevant to the evaluation of the component steps postulated by Harris: (1) the last step in each process provides a link and a relationship between two phenomena which otherwise appear to be unrelated to each other, and (2) step two of Velar Softening is simply the rule of Lenition, which is independently motivated by other facts.

The reader knowledgeable about the history of Spanish will have noted that Harris' steps parallel the historical development of the segments in question; and there can be no doubt that Harris' analysis is an insightful one with regard to what happened and why it happened. Sound changes which on the surface seem to be rather arbitrary are shown to be quite logical and predictable (with the exception of the last step) when they are viewed in terms of the underlying system.

Harris' inclusion of these steps in a synchronic grammar of Spanish seems to amount to the claim that native speakers attempt to incorporate insights such as these into their phonological grammars. That is, they not only notice that alternations are present at the surface, but in addition, they remember them in terms which make them seem less strange and more natural.

4.8.4 Segment-oriented analyses of Velar Softening and Palatalization. The preceding explanation certainly constitutes a plausible hypothesis concerning the manner in which opaque phenomena such as Velar Softening and Palatalization are internalized. However, it is clear that a good deal of subconscious 'analysis' must be done by native speakers in order to enable them to base their control of Velar Softening and Palatalization on Harris' steps. I submit that in this case, the returns do not justify the effort. That is, the benefit to the language learner derived by the explanatory value of the steps is not large enough to justify the effort of postulating them. Although no empirical test of this assertion suggests itself, I should like to claim that instead of dealing with features in controlling Velar Softening and Palatalization, the speaker-learner deals directly with the surface alternations and internalizes rules not unlike the surface statements presented in Section 4.3, which are repeated here for convenience.

$$(4.4) \quad \begin{Bmatrix} k \\ g \end{Bmatrix} \dashrightarrow \begin{Bmatrix} \theta \\ x \end{Bmatrix} / \underline{\quad} \begin{bmatrix} - \text{ cns} \\ - \text{ back} \end{bmatrix}$$

$$(4.5) \quad \begin{Bmatrix} ks \\ kt \end{Bmatrix} \dashrightarrow \begin{Bmatrix} x \\ c \end{Bmatrix} / \begin{bmatrix} \underline{\quad} \\ + \text{ native} \end{bmatrix}$$

These rules are expressed in terms of segments, rather than features. Although it would be an easy matter to translate these rules into feature notation, there seems to be little

motivation to do so. Unlike the Low-level Allophonic Process
Rules, these rules seem to be manipulating segments directly
and as atomic units, rather than changing individual properties
of those segments. If this view of Velar Softening and Palatalization is correct, it suggests that rules are of two basic types
which have been called feature-oriented and segment-oriented
throughout this section. An empirically testable prediction
which can be made concerning these two types of rule is the
claim that at more abstract levels of analysis the segment-
oriented rules predominate and that at more concrete levels,
the feature-oriented rules predominate. To the extent that
this prediction is true, the proposal to distinguish these two
types of rule is itself supported.

**4.8.5 Application of the feature-oriented versus segment-
oriented distinction to other Word-level Phonology Rules.** It
has been shown that the Low-level Allophonic Process Rules
discussed in Chapter Three are all best expressed as feature-
oriented rules. In terms of the prediction made in the preceding section, it should be the case that the Word-level Phonology
Rules tend to be segment-oriented. An examination of the
rules discussed in this chapter yields the following.
(1) Lenition is clearly feature-oriented.
(2) The structural change which inheres in Stress Assignment is clearly the addition of a feature [+ stress]; however,
the context for application is expressed largely in terms of segments and boundaries.
(3) Velar Softening, Palatalization, and Epenthesis seem to
be segment-oriented.
(4) Final -e Deletion appears to be a mixture. The deletion
of the [e] itself is clearly a segment-oriented process, whereas
the context is expressed in terms of features.
(5) Diphthongization is perhaps the most difficult case to
classify. The change itself appears to be a mixture of both
rule types. The insertion of [e] should be viewed as a
segment-oriented process. In addition to this insertion, the
original vowel /e/ or /o/ is raised to [i] or [u], and this part
of the rule is feature-oriented.[4]
The proposal to distinguish formally these two types of rule
derives some support from the above classification.

4.8.6 The formalism of segment-oriented rules. Since each
lexical entry consists of bundles of semantic, syntactic, and
phonological features, a formal device is needed to allow reference to a segment directly. I assume that segment-oriented
rules function in the following manner: a phonological grammar
includes an inventory of phonemes of the language. Each entry
in the inventory consists of a symbol and the set of features
which constitutes the definition of that segment. The effect
of a segment-oriented rule upon a phonological matrix is the
substitution of the defining features of the output segment for

those of the input segment. This formalism corresponds exactly to the claim that native speakers are manipulating segments directly rather than on a feature-by-feature basis.[5]

4.9 Conclusions. This chapter has dealt with abstract rules. In standard generative treatments of Spanish, e.g. Harris (1969), these rules have been included, along with the Low-level Allophonic Process Rules, in a single undivided phonological component. In other treatments such as 'natural' generative grammar, as represented by Hooper (1973), rules of this sort have been excluded from the phonology entirely and have assumed a lexical status.

In my view, an intermediate treatment seems best. The rules are phonological rules and are therefore included in the phonological component. However, in the light of the many differences between these rules and Low-level Allophonic Process Rules which have been pointed out throughout this chapter, it seems necessary to recognize a formal distinction between the two sets of rules.

This is done by establishing two subcomponents of the phonology: Word-level Phonology Rules and Low-level Allophonic Process Rules. This subdivision makes an empirically testable prediction concerning ordering: all Word-level Phonology Rules are ordered before the entire set of Low-level Allophonic Process Rules. If a Word-level Phonology Rule ever needs to apply to the output of a Low-level Allophonic Process Rule, then the subdivision presented here is weakened.

By way of conclusion, I should like to claim that this subdivision lends further support to the variable theory of the abstractness of lexical representations presented in Section 2.9. It is possible to claim that two speakers who produce essentially the same phonetic output have nonetheless different grammars, in that one speaker controls a particular phenomenon (e.g. Palatalization) phonologically (in terms of lexical entries such as /lakte/ and a Palatalization Rule), whereas the other speaker controls the same phenomenon lexically (in terms of underlying forms such as /leče/ for leche and /noče/ for noche which do not take cognizance of the relationship between these words and láctico and nocturno, respectively).

Whereas the grammars of all speakers, undoubtedly, contain all the Low-level Allophonic Process Rules, some Word-level Phonology Rules may be absent from the grammars of some speakers.

NOTES

1. There are difficulties associated with the assumption that word boundary occurs wherever there is a space in traditional orthography. For example, when a Spanish clitic pronoun precedes a verb, it is written as a separate word in traditional orthography (me lo das 'you give it to me') but when a clitic

follows a verb, the two elements are written as one word
(dámelo 'give it to me'). From the standpoint of linguistic
analysis, it seems most appropriate to consider that the clitic
is a separate word in both cases. Therefore, the treatment
of clitics constitutes an exception to the correlation between
word boundary and orthographic space.

2. In Chapter Six, Harris (1969) replaces the name [D] with
the phonetic name [tense] ([+ tense] equals [- D]). He says
he does this in order to 'reduce terminological strangeness',
and he does not mean to equate the feature in question with
any phonetic property. His use of the term [tense] has led
to some confusion. Harris has clarified his position in Harris
(1974). In Cressey (1970) and Cressey (1971), I present a
stronger and somewhat more generalized version of Harris'
claim that the identification of [D] is not phonetic.

3. Harris (1969) deals with American Spanish, and thus
Velar Softening converts /k/ to [s], whereas in the current
study of Castilian Spanish /k/ is converted to [θ]. The arguments presented in this section are unaffected by this difference.

4. For reasons which are beyond the scope of the present
discussion, Harris (1976) does not treat Diphthongization as
containing a raising process but rather assumes that the single
vowels are converted to diphthongs directly. According to
Harris' formulation of Diphthongization, the entire rule is
segment-oriented.

5. This formalism is taken from a similar device used by
Friedman and Morin (1971) for the operation of their computer-
ized phonological grammar tester.

CHAPTER 5

EVERYWHERE RULES

5.0 Introduction. The rules discussed in Chapter Four and Chapter Three are, for the most part, ordered rules. They apply in sequence and each rule applies to the output of the preceding rule. Once an ordered rule has applied once to any given formative, it does not reapply to that formative unless the whole set of ordered rules is reapplied to a larger speech segment which contains that formative.

We turn now to a different type of rule--the 'Everywhere Rule'. As the name implies, an Everywhere Rule applies every time its structural description is met during the course of a derivation. The entire set of Everywhere Rules applies initially as an utterance enters the phonological component. Subsequently, if an ordered rule creates a situation which matches the structural description of an Everywhere Rule, the Everywhere Rule reapplies automatically. The Everywhere Rules discussed in this chapter have been given various names in previous treatments. First, the Universal Marking Conventions discussed in SPE, Chapter 9, are Everywhere Rules, as the 'Linking' convention proposed by Chomsky and Halle (SPE:419ff.) clearly indicates. There are also language-particular Everywhere Rules, and these have usually been called Morpheme Structure Rules, or Redundancy Rules.

5.1 The theory of markedness. The first type of Everywhere Rule to be discussed is the Universal Marking Conventions. These rules are assumed to be a part of the metatheory rather than of any particular grammar, and they serve to specify the relative markedness of opposing feature values. The theory of markedness was outlined in the last chapter of SPE. The claim embodied in this theory is that, in many cases, one feature value (plus or minus) is more natural or expected than the opposite value. For example, it is claimed (SPE:406) that anterior consonants are more natural or universal than nonanterior

consonants. Because of this claim, it is necessary to associate
a higher cost to [- ant] than to [+ ant] in the representations
of consonants. This is accomplished by associating the value
[m̲ ant] 'marked for anterior' with the value [- ant] and by
associating the value [u̲ ant] 'unmarked for anterior' with the
value [+ ant], in the specification of all consonants. In lexical
entries, only the m̲ values are specified. Each m̲ specification
entails a cost, whereas u̲ values are left unspecified, and therefore entail no cost.

One type of Everywhere Rule, then, is a rule which converts
m̲ and u̲ specifications to plus and minus specifications. The
rule for the feature [anterior] is expressed as in Rule (5.28).

(5.28) [u̲ ant] --→ [+ ant]

Rule (5.28) stipulates that the unmarked value of [anterior]
is plus. By virtue of this rule, any consonant which carries
no specification for the feature [anterior] will acquire a [+ ant]
specification. Furthermore, rules such as (5.28) are deemed
automatically to entail opposite statements regarding m̲ specifications. Thus, [m̲ ant] will be converted to [- ant] by the
same rule. The operation of Rule (5.28) is illustrated in Figure
5.1, which shows how the rule applies to the lexical entry of
the word gato. (Only the consonants are determined by Rule
5.28. All vowels are [- ant], and this is specified in a separate
rule.)

Figure 5.1. Partial representation of gato 'cat' before and
after the application of Rule 5.28.

	g	a	t	o
Before Rule 5.28: [ant]	m		u	
After Rule 5.28: [ant]	-		+	

5.2 Language-particular Redundancy Rules. A second type
of Everywhere Rules are those rules frequently called Redundancy Rules. Although the Universal Marking Conventions
eliminate the need for many Redundancy Rules, Chomsky and
Halle (SPE:416) note that 'some language specific Redundancy
Rules remain'.

For example, consider the slightly different points of articulation of Spanish [ĉ] and [y]. Spanish [ĉ] is [+ coronal]
(palato-alveolar), whereas [y] is [- coronal] (palatal). Clearly,
this is an idiosyncratic feature of the Spanish language, and
not a universal correlate of the tense versus lax distinction between these two segments. Thus, the different values for the
feature [coronal] cannot be supplied by a Universal Marking
Convention. However, it would be incorrect to require that
every instance of, say, [y] be specified as [m̲ coronal] in lexical

entries. Clearly, what is required is a Redundancy Rule for Spanish which states that the unmarked value of coronal is minus in the case of an obstruent which is [- anterior, - back, - tense], but plus in the case of an obstruent which is [- anterior, - back, + tense].

In the present analysis, Redundancy Rules which apply only to Spanish are formulated using the same notation which is used for the Universal Marking Conventions. The Universal Marking Conventions and the Spanish Redundancy Rules are grouped together in a single set. The only difference between Universal Marking Conventions and Spanish Redundancy Rules is that since the latter constitute a part of the particular grammar of Spanish, they entail cost. An advantage of this procedure is that an Everywhere Rule can be formulated for Spanish in cases when it is not clear whether the rule in question expresses a universal fact or a fact about Spanish. Subsequently, by comparing the sets of Everywhere Rules developed for various languages, additional insight will be gained into the correct content of the set of Universal Marking Conventions.

In order to facilitate this sort of comparison between English and Spanish, I have taken the Marking Conventions presented in SPE as a starting point. Where one of my Everywhere Rules differs from the corresponding SPE Convention, I either (1) state that it is particular to Spanish, (2) show that it is merely a reformulation of the SPE Convention and embodies the same claims, or (3) attempt to prove that the contradictory SPE Convention is incorrect.

5.3 The operation of Everywhere Rules. As stated in Section 5.0, an Everywhere Rule applies whenever its structural description is met. There are two modes of application of Everywhere Rules. The entire set is applied initially as an utterance enters the phonological component. This application of the set of Everywhere Rules serves two functions: (1) features which are unspecified in lexical matrices are specified either as plus or minus, whichever is the contextually determined unmarked value, and (2) features which are specified with the value m in lexical matrices are specified either as plus or minus, whichever is the contextually determined marked value.

In addition to this initial application of the entire set, an Everywhere Rule applies whenever its structural description is met during the course of a derivation. This second type of application can occur in a number of ways.

(1) If a new segment is introduced by a phonological rule (e.g. the epenthetic [e] of escuela, estación, etc.), then the appropriate Everywhere Rules apply to the new segment. Thus, rules which insert segments into utterances need not specify all the feature values of the segments which they insert, but only the m specified features which define those segments in lexical matrices.

(2) If a segment is modified by a phonological rule (e.g. if
[o] is raised to [u] as in the Diphthongization Rule) and if the
new segment would have been subject to a given Everywhere
Rule had it been present in the lexical matrix, then the Everywhere Rule automatically applies to the new segment (thus the
[u] created by the Diphthongization Rule is automatically converted to [w] by the Everywhere Rule of Glide Formation).
These first two applications of Everywhere Rules are instances
of what Chomsky and Halle call 'linking'.
(3) Finally, as proposed in Section 3.1.3.1, whenever an application of a phonological rule would result in a feature configuration which violates a provision of an absolute Everywhere Rule,
that application is automatically blocked.

To conclude this section, two observations must be made concerning the ordering of Everywhere Rules. First, with respect
to the various parts of a single Everywhere Rule, the internal
ordering is disjunctive. That is, once a part of a rule has applied to any given segment, all subsequent parts of that same
rule are skipped insofar as that same segment is concerned.
Second, Everywhere Rules are not explicitly ordered with respect to each other, as are the other rules of the phonological
component. However, they do automatically apply in a certain
order whenever the application of one rule depends upon the
output of another. This intrinsic ordering of Everywhere Rules
is due to the way each rule is formulated. For example, certain Everywhere Rules apply in one way to vowels, and in another way to consonants. The feature values [+ consonantal]
and [- consonantal] appear in the context parts of these rules,
and therefore these rules cannot apply to a segment until it has
been specified as either plus or minus for the feature [conso-
nantal].

5.4 Subclassification of Everywhere Rules. Everywhere Rules
are subclassified by three factors.

5.4.1 Universal versus language-particular rules. As noted
in the previous section, rules which have been called Universal
Marking Conventions and those which have been called language-
particular Redundancy Rules are merged together here into a
single set of rules. As there are no formal differences between
the two, it is not possible to distinguish one type from the other
merely by examining the rule itself.

5.4.2 Relative versus absolute. Some Everywhere Rules
establish degrees of naturalness of opposing feature values.
These rules, such as (5.28), are relative Everywhere Rules,
and are identifiable by the inclusion of a u specification to the
left of the arrow. Other rules, however, are absolute in that
they establish a relationship between two feature specifications
which has no exceptions. For example, in Spanish, there are
no syllabic consonants such as the syllabic sonorants in the

final syllables of English butter, bitten, little, etc. Rule (5.3) is, therefore, absolute for Spanish.

(5.3)   [+ consonantal] ---→ [- syllabic]

Rule (5.3) can be read as follows: 'plus consonantal implies minus syllabic'. The inclusion of this rule in the grammar of Spanish has three consequences. (1) Any segment which is specified as [+ consonantal] by the Everywhere Rule for the feature [consonantal], will automatically be also specified [- syllabic]. (2) No [+ consonantal] segment need ever be specified in the lexicon as to the feature [syllabic]. (3) Any rule application which would create a segment specified as [+ consonantal, + syllabic] will automatically be blocked.

5.4.3 Segment-structure versus sequence-structure. Rules (5.28) and (5.3) deal exclusively with the internal feature composition of a single segment; they are segment-structure rules. Other Everywhere Rules specify a feature value only in some particular context, such as 'word-initial', 'word-final', or 'in contact with a vowel'.

For example, Rule (3.18), the Everywhere Rule of Glide Formation, includes this last context and stipulates that in the case of a high nonconsonantal segment which occurs in contact with a vowel, the unmarked value of the feature [syllabic] is minus. Rules such as (3.18) establish implications governing sequences of segments, and are thus sequence-structure rules.

5.5 The domain of Everywhere Rules. Language-particular Redundancy Rules were frequently considered to apply over the domain of a morpheme, specifying the permissible shapes of morphemes in a language. Thus, these rules were frequently called 'Morpheme Structure Rules'. In SPE, the Universal Marking Conventions are said to apply to a 'lexical entry'. In recent research (e.g. Halle 1973 and Aronoff 1976), the importance of the word has been recognized; and thus, it seems appropriate to examine the possibility that the word is the correct domain of an Everywhere Rule.

In Spanish, there are few, if any, constraints on the shape of a morpheme. Morphemes can both begin and end with sequences which are not possible in word-initial and word-final position. For example, the morpheme /abl/ of hablar ends in a consonant cluster which is never permitted at the end of a word. Although morpheme structure in Spanish is relatively unconstrained, word structure is highly constrained. Most Everywhere Rules apply over the domain of a word, and some apply over the domain of the root of a word.

5.6 A set of Everywhere Rules for Spanish. In the sections which follow, a set of Everywhere Rules for Spanish is presented and discussed. This set of rules includes both universal rules

and rules which are particular to Spanish. The rules are
grouped according to the major classes (consonant, vowel, etc.)
to which they apply. The first set deals with sequences of
consonants (Section 5.6.1). The remaining sections deal with
the various features which serve to subclassify vowels (Section
5.6.2) and sonorant consonants (Section 5.6.3), and with the
features for place and manner of articulation (Section 5.6.4).

5.6.1 Everywhere Rules which apply to consonants. The
first set of Everywhere Rules to be discussed applies to consonants as a class. Most of these rules serve to establish certain
constraints which govern sequences of Spanish consonants in
word-initial and word-final position. In addition, the sequence
C V C V is established as the most natural and least marked
sequence. Finally, an automatic property of consonants
([- syllabic]) is specified.
  Unlike the Universal Marking Conventions proposed in SPE,
the rules for Spanish have been formulated so as to apply first
to the last segment of a word. Clearly, the end of the word is
more heavily constrained in Spanish than the beginning. For
there are no consonant clusters in word-final position, and, at
the point in the derivation at which the Everywhere Rules first
apply, virtually all nouns, and adjectives end in a vowel.

  (5.1) 'no final consonant clusters'

$$[\ \ ] \longrightarrow [- \text{cns}] \ / \ \underline{\quad} \ [\text{m cns}] \ \#$$

Rule (5.1) applies to any segment, by virtue of the blank
square brackets to the left of the arrow. The rule states that
any segment which is followed directly by a segment specified
as [m cns] which is in turn followed by a word boundary (i.e.
any segment which is followed by a word-final consonant) is to
be specified as [- cns]. The rule is language-particular and it
is absolute. Although one does find marginal exceptions, such
as fórceps, chist, tórax [tóraks], none is native to Spanish.

  (5.2) '. . . C V C V sequences'

$$[\text{u cns}] \longrightarrow \begin{cases} [- \text{cns}] \ / \ \underline{\quad} \ \# & \text{(a)} \\ [\alpha \ \text{cns}] \ / \ \underline{\quad} \ [-\alpha \ \text{cns}] & \text{(b)} \end{cases}$$

Rule (5.2a) establishes minus as the unmarked value of the
feature [consonantal] in word-final position. Rule (5.2b) stipulates that for any nonfinal segment, the unmarked value for the
feature [consonantal] is minus if the following segments is
[+ cns], and vice versa.

  (5.3) 'there are no syllabic consonants'

$$[+ \text{cns}] \longrightarrow [- \text{syl}]$$

Rules (5.4) through (5.8) describe certain constraints upon word-initial consonant clusters. They are all particular to Spanish. These rules are discussed together in this section because they all express constraints upon consonant clusters. However, they apply at various points interspersed among the rules which apply to point and manner of articulation features.

(5.4) 'first member of an initial consonant cluster is nonsonorant'

$$[+ \text{ cns}] \longrightarrow [- \text{ son}] \ / \ \# \underline{\quad} [+ \text{ cns}]$$

(5.5) 'first member is neither [ĉ] nor [y]'

$$[+ \text{ cns}] \longrightarrow [- \text{ high}] \ / \ \# \left[\frac{\underline{\quad}}{- \text{ back}} \right] [+ \text{ cns}]$$

(5.6) 'first member is neither [x] nor [θ]'

$$[+ \text{ cns}] \longrightarrow [+ \text{ ocl}] \ / \ \# \left[\begin{array}{c} \underline{\quad} \\ + \text{ tns} \\ \left\{ \begin{array}{c} + \text{ back} \\ \left[\begin{array}{c} + \text{ ant} \\ + \text{ cor} \end{array} \right] \end{array} \right\} \end{array} \right] [+ \text{ cns}]$$

(5.7) 'first member is neither [t] nor [d] if second member is [l]'

$$[+ \text{ cns}] \longrightarrow [- \text{ cor}] \ / \ \# \left[\frac{\underline{\quad}}{+ \text{ ant}} \right] [+ \text{ lat}]$$

(5.8) 'first member is [s] if second member is an obstruent or a nasal'

$$[+ \text{ cns}] \longrightarrow \left[\begin{array}{c} - \text{ ant} \\ + \text{ cor} \\ - \text{ ocl} \\ + \text{ tns} \end{array} \right] \ / \ \# \underline{\quad} \left\{ \begin{array}{c} [- \text{ son}] \\ [+ \text{ nas}] \end{array} \right\}$$

Rule (5.4) specifies that the first consonant is not a sonorant, Rule (5.5) specifies that it is neither [ĉ] nor [y], Rule (5.6) specifies that it is neither [x] nor [θ], Rule (5.7) excludes [t] and [d] before [l], and Rule (5.8) specifies that if the second consonant is an obstruent or a nasal, then the first consonant must be [s]. These rules do permit [s] as the first member of a word-initial consonant cluster, even though the pattern never surfaces phonetically. The Epenthesis Rule (Section 4.1.4) adds an initial [e] to all words which, at the phonemic level, begin with the sequence /s [+ cns]/. The Epenthesis Rule must follow

Stress Assignment since the epenthetic [e] is never stressed, even when it occupies the normal position for stress (e.g. est<u>á</u>s, est<u>á</u>, see Harris 1969:141). Therefore, the Epenthesis Rule <u>must</u> be a rule of phonology, and the initial sequence /s [+ cns]/ must be allowed at the level to which the Everywhere Rules first apply.

5.6.2 Everywhere Rules which apply to all nonconsonantal segments. The next set of Everywhere Rules to be discussed has three purposes: (1) to specify the automatic properties shared by all nonconsonantal segments, (2) to specify marked and unmarked values for the features which distinguish Spanish vowels from each other, and (3) to specify some segments as glides and others as vowels.

(5.9) 'automatic features of nonconsonantals'

$$[- \text{cns}] \longrightarrow \begin{bmatrix} - \text{ lat} \\ - \text{ ant} \\ - \text{ cor} \\ - \text{ den} \\ - \text{ ocl} \\ + \text{ son} \\ - \text{ ins} \end{bmatrix}$$

Rule (5.9) establishes the automatic consequences of the specification [- cns]. These all seem universal; and, further-more, seem to derive automatically from the feature definitions themselves. Thus, the fact that all vowels are [- occlusive] is not really a fact about language but rather an inherent property of the system being used to describe language. Rules such as (5.9) must be included in the interest of mechanical viability of the system, but they are of little importance.

In SPE:408ff., the following claims are made concerning the relative naturalness of the five basic vowels. (1) The low vowel [a] is said to be the least marked vowel, and is unmarked for all the features which differentiate vowels from each other; (2) the high vowels [i] and [u] are each marked for one feature; and (3) the mid vowels [e] and [o] are the most highly marked of the basic five, being marked for two features each.

A quite different claim is made in this study concerning the relative naturalness of the five basic vowels of Spanish. How-ever, even if it can be shown that [a] should be fully unmarked as claimed by Chomsky and Halle, the rule in SPE:405 (Con-vention VIa) which makes it possible to do so, is unsatisfactory in that it constitutes a renunciation of the binary principle. In SPE, the segments [a], [i], and [u] are kept distinct solely by three different values for the feature [back]:[u] = [+ back], [i] = [- back], and [a] = [u back]. This trinary feature is used in SPE Convention VIa, in which the value <u>u</u> is deemed to contrast both with plus and with minus. The feature [back] is thus a trinary feature at this point in the derivation. Once the entire set of SPE Marking Conventions has applied, [a], [i], and [u] (and all other segments) are fully specified with binary features. However, if the binary nature of features is to be applied to the lexicon as well as to the phonology, then Convention VI (SPE:405) is not properly formulated.[1]

In considering the Spanish vowel system, there are good reasons for believing that [e], not [a] is the least marked vowel. The vowel [e] is the neutral position vowel.[2] Moreover, it is the vowel which surfaces in three instances of addition of a vowel to an underlying form. (1) The Epenthesis Rule adds a vowel in order to break up an initial cluster. Since the quality of that vowel is of no consequence, the neutral, or least marked, vowel is chosen. (2) The vowel [e] is also added to form the diphthong which is derived from some instances of stressed [e] and [o]. (3) In the morphology of nouns and adjectives, [e] is the vowel which is added to stems when the gender is not to be expressed overtly by the traditional gender vowels [a] for feminine and [o] for masculine. (For example, la noche, el combate, alegre).

Furthermore, due to the effects of a sound change rule, a significant number of Latin high vowels were lowered to mid vowels, thus giving Spanish more than the usual proportion of mid vowels. In addition, there is one context (in word-final unstressed syllable) from which high vowels are virtually excluded. These facts, taken together, suggest two things: (1) that [e] is the least marked vowel in Spanish, and (2) that mid vowels are less marked than high vowels. I, therefore, offer the hypothesis that, for Spanish at least, the unmarked value of vowel features is, in most instances, minus. This hypothesis is reflected in the following Everywhere Rules.

(5.10) 'low'

[u low] ---> [- low]

(5.11) 'back'

$$[\text{u back}] \longrightarrow \begin{cases} [+ \text{ back}] \ / \ \left[\underline{}\right] & \text{(a)} \\ \phantom{[+ \text{ back}] \ / \ } {}_{+ \text{ low}} \\ [- \text{ back}] \ / \ \left[\underline{}\right] & \text{(b)} \\ \phantom{[- \text{ back}] \ / \ } {}_{- \text{ cns}} \end{cases}$$

Rule (5.11a) expresses the hypothesis (as expressed in SPE) that in the case of low vowels, [+ back] is the unmarked value. Rule (5.11b) states, following the general hypothesis proposed earlier, that for all other nonconsonantal segments, minus is the unmarked value of the feature [back]. In SPE, it is claimed that [+ back] and [- back] are equally unmarked with respect to nonlow vowels. The alternative hypothesis presented here is supported for Spanish by the following facts. (1) The vowel [e] takes priority over all other vowels, as explained earlier, and (2) the nonlow back vowels are the only ones which never appear as theme vowels of verbs, another situation in which arbitrary use of some vowels is made.

(5.12) 'high'

$$[u \text{ high}] \longrightarrow [- \text{ high}] \ / \ \left[\underline{\hspace{1cm}} \right]_{- \text{ cns}}$$

(5.13) 'round'

$$[u \text{ rnd}] \longrightarrow \begin{cases} [- \text{ rnd}] \ / \ \left[\underline{\hspace{1cm}} \right]_{+ \text{ low}} & (a) \\ [\alpha \text{ rnd}] \ / \ \left[\underline{\hspace{1cm}} \right]_{\alpha \text{ back}} & (b) \end{cases}$$

Rule (5.13) establishes [- round] as the unmarked value of low vowels and states that in the case of nonlow vowels, the value of the feature [round] tends to agree with the value of the feature [back].

Taken together, Rules (5.10) to (5.13) establish markedness values for the five basic Spanish vowels as shown in Figure 5.2. The combinations of m and u specifications given in Figure 5.2 for each vowel constitute the feature values which are used to specify vowels in lexical entries.

Figure 5.2. Markedness values of Spanish vowel phonemes.

	i	e	a	o	u
[low]	u	u	m	u	m
[back]	u	u	u	m	m
[high]	m	u	u	u	m
[rnd]	u	u	u	u	u
markedness	1	0	1	1	2

The next Everywhere Rule to be discussed is the rule of Glide Formation which has been discussed in Section 3.5.2.1. This rule, which is Rule (5.14a) stipulates that in the case of a high nonconsonantal segment which is adjacent to a vowel, the unmarked value of the feature [syllabic] is minus. Rule (5.14b) states that in all other environments, the unmarked value of the feature [syllabic] for nonconsonantal segments is plus.

(5.14) 'Glide Formation'

$$[\text{u syl}] \longrightarrow \begin{cases} [-\text{ syl}] \;//\; \begin{bmatrix} \underline{} \\ +\text{ high} \\ -\text{ low} \end{bmatrix} V & \text{(a)} \\[20pt] [+\text{ syl}] & \text{(b)} \end{cases}$$

In addition to the features just discussed, the phonetic feature [tense] and the abstract features [strong] and [diph] apply to vowels. The unmarked values of these three features are specified in Rules (5.15) through (5.17).

(5.15) 'tense'

$$[\text{u tns}] \dashrightarrow [+\text{ tns}] \;/\; \begin{bmatrix} \underline{} \\ -\text{ cns} \end{bmatrix}$$

(5.16) 'strong'

$$[\text{u strong}] \longrightarrow [+\text{ strong}]$$

(5.17) 'diph'

$$[\text{u diph}] \longrightarrow [-\text{ diph}]$$

Rule (5.15) specifies [+ tense] as the unmarked value for Spanish vowels and Rules (5.16) and (5.17) stipulate the unmarked values for the two abstract vowel features discussed in Sections 4.3.1.1 and 4.6.3.4.4. This makes it possible to specify in the lexicon only the least natural cases; vowels which are not stressed when penultimate, and those which undergo Diphthongization will be marked for the appropriate feature in lexical entries.

5.6.3 **Everywhere Rules which apply to sonorant consonants.** Rules (5.18) through (5.26) specify the unmarked values of the features which apply to sonorant consonants and, in addition, stipulate certain automatic properties of various classes of sonorant consonants.

Rules (5.18), (5.19), and (5.20) apply to nasals. They specify minus as the unmarked value of the feature [nasal] (nasals are specified as [m nas] in the lexicon), stipulate the automatic features of nasals, and specify that /n/ is the only word-final nasal phoneme in Spanish, when what follows is a pause or a vowel.

(5.18) 'nasal'

$$[\text{u nas}] \longrightarrow [-\text{ nas}]$$

(5.19) 'automatic features of nasals'

$$[+ \text{nas}] \dashrightarrow \begin{bmatrix} + \text{son} \\ + \text{ocl} \end{bmatrix}$$

(5.20) '/n/ is the only word-final nasal'

$$[+ \text{nas}] \dashrightarrow \begin{bmatrix} + \text{ant} \\ + \text{cor} \end{bmatrix} / \underline{\quad} \# \begin{Bmatrix} || \\ V \end{Bmatrix}$$

Rules (5.21) and (5.22) apply to laterals. They specify minus as the unmarked value of the feature [lateral] and specify the automatic properties of laterals.

(5.21) 'laterals'

$$[\text{u lat}] \dashrightarrow [- \text{lat}]$$

(5.22) 'automatic features of laterals'

$$[+ \text{lat}] \dashrightarrow \begin{bmatrix} + \text{son} \\ + \text{ocl} \end{bmatrix}$$

(5.23) 'no velar laterals'

$$[+ \text{lat}] \dashrightarrow [- \text{back}]$$

(5.24) 'no labial laterals'

$$[+ \text{lat}] \dashrightarrow [+ \text{cor}] / \begin{bmatrix} \underline{\quad} \\ + \text{ant} \end{bmatrix}$$

Rules (5.23) and (5.24) have been discussed in Section 3.1.3.1. They limit the points of articulation of laterals to four possibilities: dental, alveolar, palato-alveolar, and palatal. Rule (5.24) depends upon the value of the feature [anterior] and thus must apply after Rule (5.28), which specifies the unmarked value of that feature. Rule (5.24) has been presented in this section, however, in order to discuss the special rules for laterals together.

Rules (5.25) and (5.26) deal with vibrants, which are specified as [m son] in lexical entries. Once vowels, glides, nasals, and laterals have been specified as sonorants (Rules (5.9), (5.20), and (5.22)), minus is specified as the unmarked value of the feature [sonorant]. Thus, only vibrants need be marked for the feature [sonorant]. Rule (5.26) expresses the fact, discussed earlier (Section 4.1.3), that in root-initial position, tense /r̃/ is the only vibrant which occurs.

(5.25)   'sonorant'

[u son] ---> [- son]

(5.26)   '/r̃/ is the only stem initial vibrant'

$$\begin{bmatrix} + \text{ son} \\ + \text{ cns} \\ - \text{ nas} \\ - \text{ lat} \end{bmatrix} ---> [+ \text{ tns}] \ / = \underline{\quad}$$

Rule (5.27) expresses the fact that all sonorants are automatically voiced.

(5.27)   'sonorants are voiced'

[+ son] ---> [+ voi]

5.6.4 Additional Everywhere Rules which apply to place and manner of articulation features. Some Everywhere Rules have already been presented which limit place of articulation in certain specified contexts (e.g. Rules (5.5) through (5.7) limit the point of articulation of a consonant which is a member of a word-initial consonant cluster). Other Everywhere Rules have been presented which limit the possible points of articulation of particular classes of segments (e.g. Rules (5.23) and (5.24) limit the possible points of articulation of laterals). In addition, the rules presented which deal with the tongue position of vowels (Rules (5.9) through (5.13)) deal also with point of articulation. In this section, additional rules for point of articulation and some rules governing manner of articulation are presented. In some instances, a rule discussed earlier must be modified in order to apply correctly to obstruents. In each of these cases, the rule is reformulated as the discussion progresses.

(5.28)   'anterior'

[u ant] ---> [+ ant]

It seems reasonable to assume (as do Chomsky and Halle, SPE:406) that the anterior consonants are more universal than the nonanterior consonants.

(5.29) 'back' (revision of (5.11))

$$[u \text{ back}] ---> \left\{ \begin{array}{l} [+ \text{ back}] \ / \left(\left\{ \begin{array}{l} \left[\overline{+ \text{ low}} \right] \\ \left[\begin{array}{l} - \text{ son} \\ - \text{ ant} \end{array} \right] \end{array} \right\} \right) \quad \begin{array}{l} \text{(a)} \\ \\ \text{(b)} \end{array} \\ [- \text{ back}] \qquad\qquad\qquad \text{(c)} \end{array} \right.$$

Rule (5.29) establishes the following values of [back] as the unmarked values: [+ back] is the unmarked value in the case of (a) low vowels, and (b) nonanterior obstruents, and [- back] is the unmarked value in all other cases. Part (b) of the rule serves to establish the priority of velars over palatals. In Spanish, part (b) must be limited to obstruents because there are palatal sonorant consonant phonemes (/l̃/ and /ñ/) but no velars.

(5.30) 'high' (revision of (5.12))

$$[\text{u high}] \longrightarrow \begin{cases} [-\text{ high}] \ / \ \left[\underline{}\atop{-\text{ cns}}\right] & \text{(a)} \\[2ex] [\alpha\text{ high}] \ / \ \left[\underline{}\atop{-\alpha\text{ ant}}\right] & \text{(b)} \end{cases}$$

Rule (5.30b) states that the unmarked value of the feature [high] for any given consonant is the opposite of that consonant's value for the feature [anterior]. Thus anterior consonants tend to be [- high], and nonanterior consonants tend to be [+ high].

(5.31) 'round' (revision of (5.13))

$$[\text{u rnd}] \longrightarrow \begin{cases} [-\text{ rnd}] \ / \ \begin{cases} \left[\underline{}\atop{+\text{ low}}\right] & \text{(a)} \\[2ex] \left[\underline{}\atop{+\text{ cns}}\right] & \text{(b)} \end{cases} \\[4ex] [\alpha\text{ rnd}] \ / \ \left[\underline{}\atop{\alpha\text{ back}\atop{-\text{ low}}}\right] & \text{(c)} \end{cases}$$

Rule (5.31b), which is the part of the rule which has been added for consonants, states that the unmarked value of the feature [round] is minus for all consonants.

(5.32) 'tense' (revision of (5.15))

$$[\text{u tns}] \longrightarrow \begin{cases} [+\text{ tns}] \ / \ \begin{cases} \left[\underline{}\atop{-\text{ cns}}\right] & \text{(a)} \\[2ex] \left[\underline{}\atop{-\text{ son}}\right] & \text{(b)} \end{cases} \\[4ex] [-\text{ tns}] & \text{(c)} \end{cases}$$

Rule (5.32b) states that the unmarked value of the feature [tense] is plus in the case of obstruents. Rule (5.32c) states that the unmarked value is minus in all cases not covered in cases (a) and (b) (i.e. sonorant consonants).

(5.33) 'voiced'

$$[\text{u voi}] \dashrightarrow [\alpha \text{ voi}] / \left[\underline{} \atop -\alpha \text{ tns} \right]$$

Rule (5.33) applies only to obstruents, since all sonorants have been specified as [+ voiced] by a previous rule. Rule (5.33) states that for an obstruent, the unmarked value of the feature [voiced] is the opposite of the obstruent's value for the feature [tense]. It seems that an obstruent is most easily distinguished from others by the hearer when it has either the clarity of articulation provided by tenseness, or the additional momentum provided by voicing. Thus, obstruents tend to be either [+ tense] or [+ voiced], and this tendency is expressed in Rule (5.33).

(5.34) 'coronal'

$$[\text{u cor}] \dashrightarrow \left\{ \begin{array}{ll} [\text{- cor}] / \left[\underline{} \atop {-\text{ ant} \atop -\text{ tns}} \right] & \text{(a)} \\[4ex] [\alpha \text{ cor}] / \left[\underline{} \atop {-\alpha \text{ back} \atop -\text{ ant}} \right] & \text{(b)} \\[4ex] [\text{+ cor}] & \text{(c)} \end{array} \right.$$

Rule (5.34) contains one provision which is particular to Spanish, and, in part, particular to peninsular Spanish. Part (a) states that nonanterior lax consonants tend to be noncoronal. This part of the rule selects palatal [ñ] over palato-alveolar [ǹ], palatal [y] over palato-alveolar [ĵ], and palatal [ĩ] over palato-alveolar [ì]. Once the values expressed in part (a) have been established, the more universal rule of part (b) selects palato-alveolars over palatals. This part of the rule applies to Spanish [ĉ]. Part (b) also specifies velars as noncoronal, and part (c) states that in all remaining cases, the unmarked value of coronal is plus.

(5.35) 'occlusive'

$$[\text{u ocl}] \dashrightarrow [\text{+ ocl}]$$

Rule (5.35) establishes the priority of occlusives over non-occlusives.

(5.36)   'nonocclusives do not have instantaneous release'

   [- ocl] --> [- ins]

(5.37)   'sonorants do not have instantaneous release'

   [+ son] --> [- ins]

Rules (5.36) and (5.37) are rather mechanical in nature. They
state that nonocclusives and sonorants do not have instantaneous
release. Because of the nature of the feature instantaneous release [ins] itself, only occlusive sonorants are subject to the
opposition. For the obstruent occlusives, the marked and unmarked values of this feature are given in Rule (5.38).

(5.38)   'instantaneous release'

$$[u\ ins] \longrightarrow \begin{cases} [-\ ins]\ /\ \begin{bmatrix} \underline{\quad\quad} \\ -\ ant \\ -\ back \end{bmatrix} & (a) \\ \\ [+\ ins] & (b) \end{cases}$$

Rule (5.38a) repeats the claim, made in SPE:412, that at the
palatal point of articulation, affricate stops are more usual than
nonaffricate stops, (5.38b) states that at all other points of
articulation, nonaffricate stops are more natural than affricates.

(5.39)   'dental'

$$[u\ den] \longrightarrow \begin{cases} [+\ den]\ /\ \begin{cases} \begin{bmatrix} \underline{\quad\quad} \\ +\ ant \\ +\ tns \\ -\ ocl \\ -\ son \end{bmatrix} & (a) \\ \\ \begin{bmatrix} \underline{\quad\quad} \\ +\ ant \\ +\ cor \\ -\ son \end{bmatrix} & (b) \end{cases} \\ \\ [-\ den] & (c) \end{cases}$$

Rule (5.39) establishes the total predictability of the feature
[dental] for Spanish consonants. Anterior tense fricatives are
dental ([f] and [θ]) as are anterior coronal obstruents ([t] and
[d]); all other consonants are nondental.

**5.7 Everywhere Rules and the representations of the pho-
nemes of Spanish.** Because of the Everywhere Rules, the representations of the phonemes of Spanish can be simplified

considerably, and the inventory of phonemes given as Figure 3.1 can be replaced by Figure 5.3 (p. 124), in which each segment is specified by, at most, three feature specifications.

In actual lexical entries, the representations of a given phoneme may vary from the representations given in Figure 5.3, because some of the Everywhere Rules depend upon context. For example, if the CVCV sequence is violated, as in the word múltiple, segments which are out of sequence must be specified as [m cns]. In Figures 5.4 through 5.8, representations are given for the following words: múltiple, rico, blanco, país, and escuela. The representations of some of the segments differ from the representations given for those same segments in Figure 5.3. In each instance the difference is circled in the figure, and is explained.

In the representation of múltiple (Figure 5.4), the /l/ and the /p/ must be marked for the feature [consonantal] because, starting from the end of the word and working forward, these two segments violate the CVCV sequence. In addition, the penultimate vowel must be marked for the feature [strong] since it is not stressed.

Figure 5.4. Lexical representation of múltiple.

	m	ú	l	t	i	p	l	e
[cns]		ⓜ				ⓜ		
[nas]	m							
[lat]			m				m	
[back]		m						
[high]		m			m			
[cor]	m					m		
[strong]				ⓜ				

In the representation of rico (Figure 5.5), the /r̃/ need not be marked for the feature [tense] since that feature specification will automatically be supplied by Rule (5.26).

Figure 5.5. Lexical representation of rico.

	r̃	i	k	o
[son]	m			
[ant]			m	
[back]				m
[high]		m		
[tns]	◯			

Figure 5.3. Phonemes of Spanish expressed in markedness notation.

	i	e	a	o	u	j	w	r	r̃	l	ĩ	m	n	ñ	p	t	ĉ	k	b	d	y	g	f	θ	s	x
[cns]	–	–	–	–	–	–	–	+	+	+	+	+	+	+	+	+	+	+	+	+	+	+	+	+	+	+
[syl]	+	+	+	+	+	–	–																			
[nas]												m	m	m												
[lat]										m	m															
[son]								m	m	m	m	m	m	m												
[ant]								m		m		m	m		m	m			m				m	m	m	
[low]			m																							
[back]			m	m	m		m											m				m				m
[high]	m				m	m	m																			
[rnd]				m	m		m																			
[cor]								m	m	m			m			m	m			m	m			m	m	
[tns]								m							m				m	m	m	m		m		
[ocl]															m	m	m	m	m	m						
[ins]																							m	m	m	m
[den]																										
[voi]																										

Note: The plus and minus specifications included in this inventory are not used in lexical representations. They are included here for the purpose of distinguishing every phoneme from all others in the inventory itself.

In the representation of país (Figure 5.6), there is an /e/ on the end of the word at the stage in the derivation at which the Everywhere Rules first apply (after the morphological rules have applied and before the application of any phonological rules). The /a/ must be marked for the feature [consonantal] because it is out of sequence, and the /i/ must be marked for the feature [syllabic] to prevent it from becoming a glide.

Figure 5.6. Lexical representation of país.

	p	a	i	s	e
[cns]		ⓜ			
[syl]			ⓜ		
[ant]				m	
[low]		m			
[back]					
[high]			m		
[cor]	m				
[ocl]				m	

In the representation of escuela (Figure 5.7), the diphthong [we] is represented as an /o/ (cf. escolar, escolástico), and the epenthetic [e] is not included in the representation. The /s/ need only be marked for the feature [consonantal] since /s/ is the only consonant which can occur in this environment. The underlying /o/ is marked for the feature [diph] to indicate that it undergoes the Diphthongization Rule.

Figure 5.7. Lexical representation of escuela.

	s	k	o	l	a
[cns]	ⓜ				
[lat]				m	
[ant]	◯	m			
[low]					m
[back]	◯		m		
[high]					
[ocl]	◯				
[diph]			ⓜ		

In the representation of blanco (Figure 5.8), both the /b/ and the /n/ are out of CVCV sequence, and are thus marked [m cns]. The /b/ need not be marked for the feature [coronal] because the corresponding coronal consonant /d/ cannot occur before /l/ in word-initial position.

Figure 5.8. Lexical representation of <u>blanco</u>.

	b	l	a	n	k	o
[cns]	ⓜ			ⓜ		
[nas]				m		
[lat]		m				
[ant]					m	
[low]			m			
[back]						m
[high]						
[cor]	O					
[tns]	m					

5.8 Conclusion. In this chapter, the rules which convert
from 'u versus m' notation to 'plus versus minus' notation have
been discussed. This concludes the discussion of the phonology
proper. The remaining chapter deals with morphology and presents a sample of inflectional process rules. These are the least
concrete rules which are discussed in this book, and are the
rules most closely related to the semantic aspects of utterances.

NOTES

1. I take Chomsky and Halle's use of a trinary feature to have
been an oversight on the part of the authors. Surely the purpose of the theory of markedness is not to introduce new feature values to be used in contrast with each other and with the
old values as well. As pointed out in Section 5.1, the notation
u versus m is intended solely as a shorthand method of associating cost to some specifications while allowing others to be free
of cost. The problem cited here is the same 'specious simplification' problem which existed in the older notation using zeros,
and which was pointed out in Lightner (1963). Curiously, Chomsky and Halle make the assumption (SPE:415) that the markedness notation solves the specious simplification problem 'because
there are no zeros alongside of plus and minus specifications'.
Yet their own set of rules contains a specious simplification of
precisely the sort pointed out by Lightner. For further discussion of this point, see Cressey (1970).
2. This is a good argument in favor of [e] as the least
marked vowel if one considers markedness from the standpoint
of the speaker. Chomsky and Halle (SPE:408) appear to argue
from the standpoint of the hearer, since they designate as least
marked the three vowels [i], [a], and [u] which form the sharp-
est contrasting set. For an excellent discussion of how markedness from the standpoint of the speaker and markedness from
the standpoint of the hearer differ from each other, see Guitart
(1976).

CHAPTER 6

INFLECTIONAL MORPHOLOGY

6.0 Introduction. Morphology is that branch of linguistic
science which concerns itself with the internal structure of
words. Most generative approaches have treated the morpheme
as the basic unit of form. Morphemes are then combined with
each other to form words. A particular morpheme occurs in
one or more shapes, which are termed allomorphs. Part of the
task of morphology, then, is to specify under what conditions
each allomorph of a particular morpheme occurs. As an example, consider the endings of verb forms for the imperfect indicative in Spanish. That part of the verb forms which is
uniquely associated with the meaning 'imperfect' is the sequence
ba in first conjugation verbs (hablaba, hablabas, etc.) and the
segment a in second and third conjugation verbs (comía, comías,
etc.). It can thus be said that the morpheme 'imperfect' has
the two allomorphs ba and a.
This chapter deals with the allomorphs of various noun, adjective, and verb endings, and with the rules which describe
those allomorphs. It may clarify the approach used in this
book, to contrast it with other approaches to morphology.

**6.1 American structuralist separation of morphology from
phonemics.** It has already been shown that American structural
linguists at first attempted to deal with morphology and phonemics independently of each other. It was also shown (Section 3.5.1.2) that the type of separation which the structuralists attempted to maintain, led at times to incorrect results.
For example, in the analysis of Spanish stress, it was shown
in Section 4.3.1.1 that noun stress and verb stress are determined by slightly different principles. This means that the
morphological classifications [+ noun] and [+ verb] must appear
in the phonological Stress Assignment Rule. This use of morphological information in a phonological rule would have consti-
tuted, for the structuralists, an unacceptable mixing of levels.

The structuralists were therefore unable to formulate a rule for Stress Assignment, and treated stress as phonemic.

In addition to separating morphology from phonemics, the structuralists often analyzed as morphological some phenomena which are really phonological in nature. Because of the restrictions which the structuralists placed upon phonemic analyses, they were unable to treat certain phenomena in the phonemic component. These phenomena were therefore treated in the morphology. Thus, the morpheme for the masculine singular indefinite article un was analyzed in terms of the three allomorphs /um/ [um beso], /un/ [un ombre], and /uñ/ [uñ ŷate]. As shown in Section 3.1.1.1, given the explanatory goals of generative grammar, it is incorrect to view these three pronunciations as allomorphs. The correct analysis, as presented in Section 3.1.3, has nothing to do with morphology; the various pronunciations of the final /n/ are due to the operation of a straightforward Assimilation Rule which is purely phonological in nature.

The difference between the various pronunciations of un and the two realizations of the morpheme 'imperfect' can be stated as follows. The rule which specifies the various pronunciations of un is a general rule which applies to all nasals which occur in preconsonantal position. This rule has nothing to do with un as a morpheme. On the other hand, the rule which deletes the /b/ of the imperfect morpheme applies only to that morpheme. It has been formulated exclusively to specify the alternate pronunciations of the morpheme 'imperfect' and is thus a bona fide rule of morphology.

6.2 Morphology in generative grammar. Whereas American structural linguistics attempted to maintain a strict separation between phonemics and morphology, early work in generative grammar deliberately disregarded this distinction completely. Much of what the structuralists called morphology was incorporated into the generative phonological component. More recently, generative grammar has undergone changes in the opposite direction and morphology has reemerged as an at least partially distinct component of the grammar.

In SPE:9-11, it is recognized that a small set of Readjustment Rules are needed between the output of the syntactic component and the input of the phonological component. For example, the point is made that the i of sing in the context /sing/ [+ past] acquires, by virtue of a Readjustment Rule, some feature which will eventually trigger the conversion of the i to a (sang). The Readjustment Rule which accomplishes this is essentially a rule of morphology.

In Halle (1973) and Aronoff (1976), a more detailed theory of morphology is sketched and some applications are described. This emerging theory of generative morphology deals primarily with derivational processes and the phenomena which are discussed are treated as an aspect of the lexicon. Thus, the morphological rules discussed in Halle (1973) and Aronoff (1976) apply to morphemes and thus form words. These words are then inserted into sentences. This type of morphology, as treated in the two works cited, is not part of the phonological component, and is therefore not discussed further in this book.

In my view, the Halle-Aronoff model is best suited to the analysis of derivational phenomena, whereas inflectional phenomena to my mind are best treated in a subcomponent of the phonology. This chapter, then, deals with inflectional phenomena, and is viewed as a part of the phonological component.

6.3 **Inflectional versus derivational morphology.** In the previous section, it was claimed that derivational phenomena should be analyzed as part of the lexicon, whereas inflectional phenomena should be treated in a subcomponent of the phonology. The distinction between derivational and inflectional morphology must now be defined more exactly and the rationale for treating these two types of morphology in two distinct components must be explained.

Derivational morphology deals with additions to a lexical root which determine the part of speech of the resultant word. Thus, amar 'love (verb)', amor 'love (noun)', and amoroso 'loving (adj.)' are all derived from a common root am. Before lexical insertion can take place, the syntactic category of the word must be determined. In some parts of a syntactic tree, a noun must be inserted; in others, a verb. Thus, the rules which form nouns, verbs, and adjectives must apply to a root before lexical insertion occurs. Therefore, it seems appropriate to consider derivational morphology to be a part of the lexicon.

Inflectional morphology, on the other hand, deals with affixes which express, for example, the gender and number of an adjective or the tense, person, and number of a verb. Unlike derivational processes, inflectional processes can only take place after a lexical item is inserted into an actual sentence. To take a specific example, consider the person-number ending of a conjugated verb. The features for person and number are copied from the subject of the sentence, and therefore cannot be determined before the verb is inserted into a particular sentence.[1] This fact is the primary motivation for my decision to consider inflectional morphology to be a part of the phonological component.

6.4 **Morphological rules versus phonological rules.** I have decided to treat inflectional morphology as a subcomponent of the phonology. This morphological subcomponent adds inflectional endings to lexical stems, thus forming the systematic phonemic representation of an utterance. In this section, I attempt to establish explicit criteria for the classification of a rule as either morphological or phonological.

I have already stated in Section 6.1 that if a rule is formulated exclusively for the purpose of accounting for the different shapes

of a particular morpheme, then it is a morphological rule.
Other criteria for inclusion in the morphological subcomponent
are the following.
(1) All rules which spell out the shape or shapes of a morpheme are morphological rules, for example, the rules which
specify the gender vowels of nouns and adjectives. (2) If the
context of a rule includes a feature which has semantic content,
and if the change effected by the rule can serve as the physical signal of that semantic feature, then the rule may be considered morphological unless considerations of ordering dictate
otherwise. An example of this sort of rule is Past Raising,
which is discussed in Section 6.6.1.2.4.
This second criterion is not to be considered absolute. Past
Raising meets the test, and is therefore a 'potential' morphological rule. Since, in this case, there is no compelling reason
to consider Past Raising a phonological rule, I conclude that
Past Raising is a morphological rule. In some instances, it may
appear that the test described in criterion (2) is at least partially met; however, there may be other factors which dictate
that the rule in question be ordered among the phonological
rules. In the sections which follow, various aspects of the inflectional morphology of nouns, adjectives, and verbs are discussed. In the course of the discussion, a number of rules
are formulated. Some of these rules are morphological; some
are phonological. In the case of phonological rules which appear
to meet criterion (2), reasons are given for the classification of
the rules as phonological rather than morphological.

6.5 Inflection of nouns and adjectives.

In the morphology of
nouns and adjectives, one or two morphemes may follow the stem.
The first morpheme is either an overt gender marker or an /e/;
the second, if present, is the plural morpheme /s/. It has been
shown in detail in Section 4.5.2.1 that the plural morpheme need
not be characterized in terms of allomorphs. The single segment
/s/ is sufficient for the analysis of all plurals. I turn now to
the first post-stem morpheme, the gender inflection.
All Spanish nouns are marked for gender in the lexicon. In
some instances, the gender correlates with the semantic category
of sex: hijo (masculine gender) 'son', hija (feminine gender)
'daughter'. In most cases, however, the gender is an arbitrary
morphological feature devoid of any semantic content: caso
(masculine gender) 'case', casa (feminine gender) 'house'.
As the above examples show, when gender is marked overtly,
masculine gender surfaces as /o/ and feminine gender surfaces
as /a/. This applies to all nouns and adjectives which have
overt gender morphemes: niño pequeño 'small boy', niña
pequeña 'small girl'. There are, in addition, many nouns and
adjectives which show no overt marking for gender. Typically,
these words end (phonetically) either with a consonant or an
/e/. In the following examples, the articles (el for masculine
and la for feminine) are the only overt markings of the gender:

el hombre feliz 'the happy man', la noche triste 'the sad night', la virtud 'virtue', el ataud 'the coffin'. There are also some outright exceptions which must be marked in the lexicon, such as: la mano 'the hand' and el poema 'the poem'.

It has been shown in Section 4.5.2, that nouns such as virtud and ataud and adjectives such as feliz, which end in a consonant at the phonetic level, are represented with a final /e/ at the systematic phonemic level. Thus, the endings of all regular nouns and adjectives fall into two categories: those which are overtly marked for gender end with /o/ (masculine) or /a/ (feminine), and all others end with /e/. It must be noted that nouns which end with /e/ still require an inherent gender feature specification in the lexicon, so that the correct form of the article and any overtly marked adjectives can be generated. Thus, in the lexicon, all nouns are marked with respect to two features: [± masculine] and [± overt gender]; adjectives are all marked in the lexicon with respect to the feature [± overt gender] and acquire a specification for the feature [masculine] by a transformational rule which copies this feature specification from the noun onto the adjective.

All regular nouns and adjectives are entered in the lexicon without the final vowel /o/, /a/, or /e/. These final vowels are not part of the idiosyncratic form which uniquely characterizes each lexical item; they are automatic reflexes of the features introduced in the preceding paragraph. Since the lexicon should include only aspects of lexical structure which do not conform to regular principles, these vowels must not be included in the lexical entries.

Lexical entries for some of the examples discussed earlier, therefore, have the following form: /kas/ [+ N, - masculine, + overt gender], /trist/ [+ Adj, - overt gender], /ombr/ [+ N, + masculine, - overt gender], /pekeñ/ [+ Adj, + overt gender].

In terms of tree structure, the features and the actual stems are related to each other as shown in Figure 6.1, which represents the plural form casas 'houses'.

Figure 6.1. Surface syntactic representation of the noun casas.

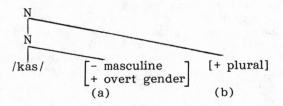

(a)   (b)

In Figure 6.1, the bundles of features (a) and (b) are adjoined to the stem in a manner which will be interpreted by the morphology as follows. Since bundles (a) and (b) derive from $\underline{N}$ nodes, they are considered to be inside the word boundary which follows this entire word. In addition, the label $\underline{N}$ is associated with the entire configuration. The string which corresponds to the tree represented in Figure 6.1 is the following.

$$\underset{N}{\left[\text{\# kas} \begin{bmatrix} -\text{ masculine} \\ +\text{ overt gender}\end{bmatrix} [+\text{ plural}] \text{ \#}\right]}_N$$

The morphological rule given as Rule (6.1) serves to supply the gender inflections of nouns and adjectives.

$$(6.1)\quad \begin{bmatrix} \alpha \text{ masculine} \\ <+ \text{ overt gender} > \end{bmatrix} \dashrightarrow \begin{bmatrix} + \text{ syllabic} \\ \\ < \begin{bmatrix} + \text{ back} \\ - \alpha \text{ low} \end{bmatrix} > \end{bmatrix}$$

Other formulations are, no doubt, possible, but Rule (6.1) seems reasonably straightforward. Its effect is to add a vowel to the end of every noun and adjective. If the stem in question is not [+ overt gender] then the only feature supplied by Rule (6.1) is the feature [+ syllabic]. As shown in Section 5.6.2, any [+ syllabic] segment which is not marked for any other feature is specified as an /e/ by Everywhere Rules (5.10) through (5.13).

If a stem to which Rule (6.1) applies is specified as [+ overt gender] then Rule (6.1) adds the features [+ back, + low] in the case of a feminine stem and [+ back, - low] in the case of a masculine stem. Once again, Everywhere Rules (5.10) through (5.13) specify these segments as /a/ and /o/, respectively.

In addition to applying to nouns and adjectives, Rule (6.1) applies to certain past participle endings which are subject to gender inflection (la casa fue vendida por Juan 'The house was sold by John').

The only other rule of inflectional morphology which applies to noun and adjective stems is the rule which introduces the plural morpheme /s/, if the feature [+ plural] is present. This rule is formulated as Rule (6.2).

$$(6.2)\quad [+\text{ plural}] \dashrightarrow s \; / \; \underline{\quad} \; \Big]_{N,\, Adj}$$

Rules (6.1) and (6.2) are completely straightforward rules which spell out the inflectional morphemes of nouns and adjectives. No other morphological rules are required, since there are no allomorphs.

We turn now to the verb system, which is considerably more complex.

6.6 **Inflection of Spanish verbs.** Spanish verbs have inflectional endings which reflect tense, aspect, mood, person, number, and sometimes gender. Regular verbs have been analyzed in the generative framework quite thoroughly in Harris (1969). Harris' analyses are all accepted as valid, and are sketched in the sections which follow in order to lay a foundation for the analysis of certain types of irregular verb forms. With the exception of the preterite tense forms, Harris' analyses of regular Spanish verb forms are quite straightforward, noncontroversial, and require little discussion. His analyses of these verb forms are presented briefly in Section 6.6.1. The preterite tense is discussed at greater length in Section 6.6.2, and an analysis of some irregular verb forms is set forth in Section 6.6.3.

6.6.1 **Harris' analyses of regular verb forms other than preterite.** In this section, Harris' treatment of all regular verb forms except the preterite is sketched briefly.

At the level of syntactic surface structure, the verb form amábamos is represented as shown in Figure 6.2.

Figure 6.2. Syntactic surface structure representation of amábamos.

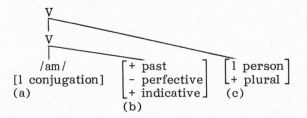

Feature bundle (a) is the stem of the verb, and is introduced into a tree by the general rule of lexical insertion, bundle (b) is generated in the phrase structure component as part of the auxiliary, and bundle (c) is introduced by a transformational rule which establishes agreement of person and number between the verb and the subject of the sentence.

6.6.1.1 **The inflectional morphemes of verb forms as generated by the Spellout Rules.** Just as in the case of nouns and adjectives, the morphological Spellout Rules replace the feature bundles shown in Figure 6.2 with morphemes. One such rule, (6.3), spells out the 'theme vowel' which immediately follows the stem in most verb forms (/am + a + mos/, /kom + e + mos/, /bib + i + mos/). Although the theme vowel is subsequently deleted from some forms (amo, como, vivo) and modified in some instances, it is initially spelled out as /a/ for first conjugation, /e/ for second conjugation, and /i/ for third conjugation.

(6.3) $\emptyset \longrightarrow \left\{ \begin{array}{l} a \ / \ [1 \text{ conjugation}] \\ e \ / \ [2 \text{ conjugation}] \\ i \ / \ [3 \text{ conjugation}] \end{array} \right\}$ ___

Rule (6.3) inserts a theme vowel immediately after the verb stem. By convention, every morphological spellout rule inserts a morpheme boundary between the new morpheme which it spells out and any other morphemes which were present before the application of the rule. Thus, the output of Rule (6.3), as it applies to the tree given in Figure 6.2, is the following:

$$\left[\# = am + a \left[\begin{array}{l} + \text{ past} \\ + \text{ perfective} \\ + \text{ indicative} \end{array} \right] \left[\begin{array}{l} 1 \text{ person} \\ + \text{ plural} \end{array} \right] \# \right]_V$$

Other spellout rules replace the tense-aspect bundle with a morpheme (/ba/ in the case of the example used here), and the person-number bundle with another morpheme (/mos/ in this instance).

Rule (6.3) illustrates how the spelling out of verb inflections takes place. In the interest of brevity, formulated spellout rules for the entire verb paradigm are not presented here. The results of the spellout rules inherent in Harris' analyses of regular present tense verb forms are given as Figure 6.3.[2] Figure 6.4 shows the underlying representation of selected additional forms which constitute the basis for my analysis of irregular forms as discussed in Section 6.6.3.

Figure 6.3. Underlying representations of present indicative verb forms.

am + a + o	kom + e + o	un + i + o
am + a + s	kom + e + s	un + i + s
am + a	kom + e	un + i
am + a + mos	kom + e + mos	un + i + mos
am + a + is	kom + e + is	un + i + is
am + a + n	kom + e + n	un + i + n

Figure 6.4. Underlying representations of selected verb forms.

Infinitive:	am + a + re	kom + e + re	un + i + re
Participle:	am + a + to	kom + e + to	un + i + to
Imperfect 1st person plural:	am + a + ba + mos	kom + e + ba + mos	un + i + ba + mos
Future 1st person plural:	am + a + re # e + mos	kom + e + re # e + mos	un + i + re # e + mos

6.6.1.2 Modifications of the inflectional morphemes. There are a number of differences between the underlying representations of verb forms (Figures 6.3 and 6.4) and the actual phonetic forms. In Harris (1969) a number of rules are presented which convert these underlying representations to the surface phonetic forms. One of these rules, the rule which deletes the word-final /e/ of infinitives, has already been discussed in Section 4.3.1.4. Although Final e Deletion was primarily formulated to apply to nouns and adjectives, it applies to the infinitive as well, since the infinitive is subject to pluralization in the same manner as are nouns and adjectives, e.g. el andar, los andares. Other modifications of the underlying representation are discussed in the sections which follow, and in some instances, a rule is given.

6.6.1.2.1 Theme Vowel Deletion. In the first person singular of the present indicative, and throughout the present subjunctive, the theme vowel is deleted by a rule which can tentatively be formulated as Rule (6.4).

$$(6.4) \quad V \longrightarrow \emptyset \; / \; + \; \underline{\quad} \; + \begin{bmatrix} V \\ u \; \text{TVD} \end{bmatrix}$$

Rule (6.4), as formulated, deletes any vowel which is both preceded and followed by morpheme boundary if the following segment is a vowel, and is not marked for the feature [TVD]. The feature [TVD] is a special exception feature which allows a vowel so marked not to trigger the deletion of a preceding theme vowel. In Harris (1969:81ff.), the feature [tense] was used as a diacritic for the same purpose. However, since the publication of Harris (1969), it has been discovered that the various uses of the feature [tense] cannot be maintained in any consistent fashion. Thus, [tense] as a phonological feature of Spanish vowels has been replaced by a small set of unrelated' diacritics.

6.6.1.2.2 Lowering of i to e. Another modification suffered by theme vowels is the lowering of the /i/ of third conjugation when it is unstressed and in the final syllable of the word. This rule lowers any unstressed high vowel in the last syllable of a word, and is a quite general rule in Spanish. There are exceptions to this rule, such as casi and tribu, but there are very few. Any exception to a rule must be specified as such in the lexicon, using a special exception feature. Thus, casi and tribu and other exceptions to Lowering must be specified as [- Lowering].

6.6.1.2.3 Lenition. The participle ending of regular verbs is [do]. Harris, however, assumes that the underlying form is /to/. This analysis has already been discussed in Section

4.4.2.1 and is commented on further in Section 6.6.3.1. The
rule which converts the /t/ to a [d] in regular forms is the
rule of Lenition, which laxes a single tense occlusive obstruent
in intervocalic position in [+ native] words.

6.6.1.2.4 Past Raising. In all past forms of second and
third conjugation verbs, the /e/ theme vowel is raised to /i/.
This rule is formulated as Rule (6.5).

(6.5) $\left[\begin{array}{c} V \\ - \text{low} \end{array} \right]$ ---> [+ high] / ___ + [+ past]

Rule (6.5) raises a mid vowel[3] if it precedes a morpheme
which is marked [+ past]. As mentioned earlier, Past Raising
is a morphological rule. In the preterite tense, the nosotros
form /komimos/ differs from the present indicative nosotros
form /komemos/ only by virtue of the effect of Past Raising.
The /e/ versus /i/ opposition thus serves, in this instanc ?,
as the only indication of the tense of the verb in sei .ences
like comemos a las siete 'we eat at seven' and comimos a las
siete 'we ate at seven'. Therefore, it seems necessary that the
two verbs be represented at the systematic phonemic level as
/komemos/ and /komimos/, which means that Past Raising must
be a morphological rule.

6.6.1.2.5 The 'imperfect' morpheme. Harris (1969:76) proposes a rule, formulated as Rule (6.6), which deletes the b of
the imperfect morpheme when it is preceded by i. Since this
rule follows the application of Past Raising, the rule of b-
Deletion applies to all second and third conjugation forms.[4]

(6.6) b ---> Ø / i + ___

Since this rule has been formulated only for the purpose of
accounting for the variant pronunciations of the 'imperfect'
morpheme, it is a morphological rule.

6.6.1.2.6 Allomorphs of the vosotros ending. Phonetically,
the vosotros ending of most tenses is [js] ([aßlájs]). In the
preterite paradigm, the ending is [stejs] ([aßlástejs]), and for
imperative forms the ending is [d] ([aßlad]). In Harris (1974c),
an analysis of these forms is given in terms of an underlying
/dis/ ending for [2 person, + plural].
Although Harris' underlying form is converted to the phonetic
surface shapes by rules which are straightforward and well
motivated, a less abstract analysis in terms of allomorphs seems
preferable to me.
In the first place, the proposed underlying form /dis/ is
radically different from the phonetic shape [js]. Secondly,
since the only other true imperative form (the tú form) does
not have the regular tú-form person-number ending (/s/), it

seems reasonable to assume that the imperative forms lack the usual person-number endings. Specifically, I shall assume that the imperative tense does not manifest any ending for second person singular (habla) and includes a special /d/ ending for second person plural (hablad).

Having separated the rest of the tenses from the imperative in this manner, the most straightforward representation of the vosotros forms of the other tenses is /is/. Since the /i/ of this ending does not trigger Theme Vowel Deletion, it must be specified as [m TVD].[5]

Since it has been decided not to derive [js] and [d] from a single underlying representation, the two vosotros allomorphs must be introduced directly by a spellout rule. This rule is given as (6.7), which also spells out the preterite allomorph for vosotros.

$$(6.7) \quad \begin{bmatrix} 2 \text{ person} \\ + \text{ plural} \end{bmatrix} \longrightarrow \begin{cases} d \ / \ [+ \text{ imperative}] & \_\_ \ (a) \\ stejs \ / \begin{bmatrix} + \text{ past} \\ + \text{ perfective} \end{bmatrix} & (b) \\ is & (c) \end{cases}$$

Rule (6.7c) applies to all tenses not specifically mentioned in parts (a) and (b) of the rule.

There is an important distinction between these allomorphs of [2 person, + plural] and the two variant pronunciations of 'imperfect'. In the analysis of the 'imperfect' morpheme, one of the pronunciations ([a]) was derived from the other ([ba]). This means that although a morphological rule is needed to specify the variants, the phonological relationship between them is maintained. In the case of the vosotros morpheme, however, the attempt to maintain a phonological relationship between the allomorphs has been abandoned completely, and the allomorphs are considered totally distinct ways of pronouncing the same bundle of semantic features.

6.6.2 **The Spanish preterite tense.** The preterite tense has been the subject of considerable confusion, largely because it does not manifest the clear division into 'stem + theme vowel + person marker' which the other tenses seem to follow. In evaluating various attempts to deal with the preterite forms, one must bear in mind the analytic principle enunciated several times throughout this book, which was called the condition of naturalness by Postal (1964:55ff.).

For the purposes of this section, a corollary of the natural-ness condition can be expressed as follows: Given two compet-ing analyses of a form or of a set of forms, the greater burden of proof rests with the proponent of the analysis involving underlying forms which are least similar to the phonetic shape of the forms under analysis. Of course, if similarity to the phonetic shape were the only criterion for evaluating underlying

forms, then all underlying forms would be the same as the phonetic forms, and the concept of an underlying form would cease
to exist.

In this section, three different analyses of the preterite are
sketched. In each case, some justification is offered for the
differences between the underlying forms proposed and the phonetic shapes of the forms. Usually, this justification takes the
form of an argument to the effect that the underlying forms
simplify the grammar of the verb system as a whole.

Since all three analyses to be discussed are based upon
American Spanish, they exclude the vosotros forms. The
vosotros forms are therefore not considered in the sections
which follow. The correct analysis of the vosotros forms for
preterite is simple. A special vosotros ending for preterite is
introduced (see Rule 6.7) and combines with the stem and theme
vowel in a perfectly straightforward manner.

6.6.2.1 The phonetic forms. The phonetic forms of the
preterite tense paradigm are given in Figure 6.5.

Figure 6.5. Phonetic representations of preterite forms.

a - mé	ko - mí	u - ní
a - más - te	ko - mís - te	u - nís - te
a - mó	ko - mjó	n - njó
a - má - mos	ko - mí - mos	u - ní - mos
a - má - ron	ko - mjé - ron	u - njé - ron

As various possible analyses are considered, several problematical aspects of the preterite forms should be borne in mind.
First, by far the most irregular aspect of the preterite forms
is the final stress on first and third person singular forms.[6]
Second, another problematical feature is the absence of the
theme vowel in various cases. Third, the endings of most of
the forms differ from the person-number endings associated
with the other tenses.

6.6.2.2 William Bull. The first analysis to be discussed
appears in Bull (1965). Bull segments all verb forms into
three parts: stem, tense-mode-aspect marker, and person-
number ending. In Bull's analysis, the theme vowel, if present,
is considered a part of the tense-mode-aspect marker. Bull's
analysis is given in Figure 6.6.

Following a tradition common in American structural linguistics, Bull represents each verb form as a string of morphemes.
Each verb in a paradigm is thought to have the same number
of morphemes, and if no morpheme surfaces in a given 'slot',
the analyst posits a zero (∅) morpheme, as Bull has done in
the first and third person singular forms of the preterite. In
addition, one notes that, since morphology and phonemics were

Figure 6.6. Bull's analysis of preterite tense forms.

am + é + Ø	kom + í + Ø	un + í + Ø
am + a + ste	kom + i + ste	un + i + ste
am + ó + Ø	kom + ió + Ø	un + ió + Ø
am + a + mos	kom + i + mos	un + i + mos
am + aro + n	kom + iero + n	un + iero + n

thought to be separate, Bull's analysis is quite concrete and is orthographically oriented, even to the point of representing stress in exactly those forms which require a written accent mark and omitting stress in all other cases.

Within the constraints of the structuralist framework, Bull has achieved considerable descriptive adequacy as regards the third part of each form. With the exception of /ste/ for the tú forms, the morphemes which Bull (1965:118ff.) has posited for person-number are the same ones which he posits for all other tenses. The main problem in Bull's analysis is in the middle slot. In commenting on his analysis, Bull states that 'the tense-mode-aspect slot is a mixture of debris left over from Latin. Nothing much can be done with the conglomeration of parts of slot two; they have to be memorized'.[7]

An evaluation of an analysis of the preterite tense can be made in terms of how many of the problems posed in the previous section are adequately answered. Bull's analysis leaves the following questions unanswered: (a) Why do the first and third person singular forms have final stress? (b) Why does the tense-mode-aspect slot have so many different allomorphs?

In addition, some regular aspects of these forms are ignored in Bull's analysis. For example, the sequence /ro/ occurs in all third person plural forms, yet Bull has not attributed this sequence to the ending. In addition, the segment /i/ occurs as the first segment of all second and third conjugation endings, and /a/ occurs as the first segment of three out of five of the first conjugation endings, yet these facts are not mentioned by Bull, nor are they accounted for in his analyses.

6.6.2.3 Stockwell, Bowen, and Martin. In another structuralist attempt to analyze the preterite, Stockwell, Bowen, and Martin (1965) divide the forms into four parts: 'stem, theme vowel, tense-aspect marker, and person-number ending'. Their analysis is shown in Figure 6.7. Like the Bull analysis, the Stockwell, Bowen, and Martin (SBM) analysis is based upon segmentation of the physical data without any attempt at abstraction. SBM recognize the theme vowel as a separate entity; and, in this respect, their analysis is superior to Bull's. However, the SBM tense-aspect marker suffers from the same defect attributed to Bull's 'tense-mode-aspect marker': there are so many allomorphs, and the allomorphs are so different from each other, that it is difficult to discern any relationship

between form and meaning. Since a form-meaning correlation
is the essential factor in a morphological analysis, it is difficult to view either Bull's analysis or SBM's as plausible.

Figure 6.7.   Stockwell, Bowen, and Martin's analysis of
preterite tense forms.

am + Ø + é + Ø	kom + Ø + í + Ø	un + Ø + í + Ø
am + a + ste + Ø	kom + i + ste + Ø	un + i + ste + Ø
am + Ø + ó + Ø	kom + j + ó + Ø	un + j + ó + Ø
am + a + Ø + mos	kom + i + Ø + mos	un + i + Ø + mos
am + a + ro + n	kom + je + ro + n	un + je + ro + n

Of the two analyses, SBM's is slightly better. However,
each analysis entails some arbitrary decisions. An examination
of one difference between the two analyses may shed some
light on the main characteristic of the preterite which both
analysts have failed to perceive. Bull analyzed the sequence
/ste/ as a person-number ending; SBM analyzed this same sequence as a tense-mode-aspect marker. Each decision seems
arbitrary, yet each analysis seems partially correct. The fault
lies in the assumption that tense-mode-aspect and person-
number must be separate morphemes. When one examines the
verb inflection endings of Spanish, one finds that /ste/ is never
associated with any person except second person and is never
associated with any tense other than preterite. When a native
speaker of Spanish hears a verb form which ends with /ste/,
he will, without a doubt, immediately assume that the form is
a second person singular preterite form, even if he has never
heard the particular verb root before. The inescapable conclusion is that /ste/ is a spellout of all the features: [+ past,
+ perfective, 2 person]. Although the evidence is not as
dramatic in other parts of the preterite paradigm, it is clear
that /ron/ also stands as an indivisible marker of person-
number and tense-aspect. This merger into one morpheme of
feature configurations which are spelled out separately in the
rest of the verb paradigm is, in my view, the most important
insight introduced by the next analyst to be discussed.

6.6.2.4   James Harris. Harris (1969) divides the forms into
three parts: stem, theme vowel, and special person-number
endings for the preterite. His analysis is shown in Figure 6.8.
Unlike the American structuralist analyses, Harris' analysis is
not based upon simple segmentation of the surface forms. Each
inflectional ending is initially spelled out as shown in Figure
6.8, and modifications which are needed to derive the surface
forms are described by morphological and phonological rules.
For example, Past Raising (Rule 6.5) converts all the second
conjugation theme vowels to /i/.

Figure 6.8. Harris' analysis of preterite tense forms.

am + a + i	kom + e + i	un + i + i
am + a + ste	kom + e + ste	un + i + ste
am + a + u	kom + e + u	un + i + u
am + a + mos	kom + e + mos	un + i + mos
am + a + ron	kom + e + ron	un + i + ron

Once Past Raising has applied, seven of the fifteen forms require no further rules other than the completely regular application of the stress rule: [amáste], [amámos], [amáron],
[komíste], [komímos], [uníste], [unímos]. Harris has proposed
a quite straightforward rule which accounts for the conversion
of the theme vowel to [jé] in [komjéron] and [unjéron]. This
leaves only the first and third person singular forms to be explained. Since Harris' analysis of these forms constitutes the
basis for my analysis of irregular preterites (see Section
6.6.3.3), his rules for the derivation of [amé], [amó], [komí],
and [komjó] must be examined more closely.
Complete derivations for these four forms are given in Figure
6.9.

Figure 6.9. Derivations of first and third person singular
preterite forms.

	am+a+i	am+a+u	kom+e+i	kom+e+u
Past Raising:			i	i
Theme Vowel Deletion:	–	–	–	–
Stress Assignment:	á	á	í	í
A-Assimilation:	é	ó		
High Deletion:	Ø	Ø	Ø	
Stress Shift:				i ú
Lowering:				ó
Glide Formation				j
	[amé]	[amó]	[komí]	[komjó]

Note: The hyphen (-) in a derivation indicates that the rule
listed to the left fails to apply to the segment under
which the symbol appears.

As shown in the derivations, the first rule which applies is
Past Raising. After the application of Past Raising, the second
and third conjugation forms are identical; and thus the third
conjugation forms are not discussed nor included in Figure 6.9.
Since the stress falls on the endings, rather than on the stems,
these forms must not undergo Theme Vowel Deletion. Although
this is not Harris' original analysis, I assume that the special
preterite endings for first and third person are marked with
the special diacritic [m TVD].[8] Next, Stress Assignment

applies, assigning stress to the theme vowel in each of the four forms.

Four additional rules are formulated by Harris for the analysis of these forms. These rules have the following effects. A-assimilation raises an /a/ to /e/ if followed by /i/ and to /o/ if followed by /u/. High Deletion deletes a high vowel when it agrees with the preceding vowel as to the feature [back]. These two rules together convert [am + á + i] and [am + á + u] to [amé] and [amó], respectively. These two rules are motivated by virtue of applications outside the verb system. For example, these rules account for ai ~ e alternations in pairs such as laico--lego, and au ~ o alternations in pairs such as áureo--oro. In each of these pairs, the first word is a learned ([- native]) word which does not undergo A-assimilation and High Deletion. The other word, a native word, is derived from an underlying form containing a followed by a high vowel. The second word in each pair undergoes these two rules; and the existence of these pairs provides evidence in favor of the rules, which is independent of the analysis of the preterite.

High Deletion also deletes the final [i] of [kom + í + i]. The other two rules proposed by Harris are a Stress Shift rule and a Lowering rule, which apply to [kom + í + u] yielding [komió]. Glide Formation then yields [komjo]. Of all the rules used in the derivation of preterite forms, only Stress Shift and Lowering can be said to lack independent motivation. For further discussion of all these rules, and exact formulations, see Harris (1969:79ff.). Although Harris' analysis of preterite forms is more abstract than his analysis of the other verb forms, it has been repeatedly pointed out that the forms themselves are complex and irregular and have presented difficulty to all who have grappled with them.[9]

6.6.3 Analysis of some irregular verb forms. In a generative phonology, a verb is considered irregular, not simply because its paradigms differ from those of other verbs, but only if the differences cannot be explained in terms of general rules. For example, as shown in Section 4.7, the so-called 'radical changing' verbs (pensar/pienso, poder/puedo) are not irregular verbs in the generative framework. Instead, they are described as containing vowels which are specially marked to undergo Diphthongization. Once these verbs, and certain others, are disposed of, there are still many verb forms which must be accounted for in terms of special exception features associated with the lexical entries of the verb stems in question. It must be remembered that a decision as to whether or not a given verb requires a special marking in the lexicon depends, in part, upon the set of rules which are accepted as correct for the analysis of regular forms. Specifically, in the case of Spanish verbs, the morphological spellout rules and the morphological and phonological rules which convert the underlying forms of regular verbs to their phonetic manifestations constitute the proper basis for any work with irregular verbs. For this reason, I have used the rules and derivations proposed in Harris (1969) as a starting point. This makes it possible to determine in what ways the underlying forms and/or rules used in the analysis of irregular verbs differ from the underlying forms and rules of regular verbs. Only in this way can the special properties of irregular verb forms be properly evaluated.

In the sections which follow, it is shown that, among Spanish irregular verb forms, there is a large group whose irregularities can be at least partially explained in terms of the notion of 'athematicity'. An athematic verb form is one which lacks the theme vowel at a point in the derivation when it would normally be present. From the standpoint of rules, an athematic verb form undergoes Theme Vowel Deletion (Rule 6.4) in an unusual manner. Either the verb form undergoes Theme Vowel Deletion although it does not meet the normal structural description for application of the rule, or the verb form undergoes Theme Vowel Deletion at an earlier point in the derivation than is usually the case.

6.6.3.1 Athematic past participles. One case of athematicity, pointed out in Foley (1965), is the set of irregular past participles. If the underlying form of the past participle ending is assumed to be /to/, as suggested in Sections 4.4.1 and 6.6.1.2.3, then the irregular forms listed in Figure 6.10 can be explained by assuming that the theme vowel has been deleted from these forms before the application of the rule for voicing of intervocalic stops and certain other phonological rules. In order to explain completely the phonetic shapes of many of these past participles, additional rules are required.

Figure 6.10. Athematic past participles.

Infinitive	Underlying form of past participle	Phonetic form
abrir	/aper + i + to/	[aƀjérto]
cubrir	/cuper + i + to/	[cuƀjérto]
morir	/mor + i + to/	[mwérto]
volver	/bolb + e + to/	[bwélto]
soltar	/solt + a + to/	[swélto]
escribir	/scrip + i + to/	[eskríto]
ver	/bid + e + to/	[bísto]
poner	/pos + e + to/	[pwésto]
decir	/dik + i + to/	[díĉo]
hacer	/ak + e + to/	[éĉo]
romper	/rup + e + to/	[řóto]

In addition, some of the underlying forms proposed are not the most obvious ones. For a complete discussion of these underlying forms and rules which apply to them, see Foley (1965) and Harris (1969). As an illustration, derivations for the regular forms and the irregular forms muerto and dicho are given in Figure 6.11.

Figure 6.11. Derivations of amado, muerto, and dicho.

	am+a+to	mor+i+to	dik+i+to
Theme Vowel Deletion:	–	∅	∅
Stress Assignment:	á	ó	í
Palatalization:			č
Diphthongization:		wé	
Lenition:	d		
Fricativization:	đ		
	[amáđo]	[mwérto]	[díčo]

As these derivations show, the analysis of irregular past participles is carried out in terms of a lexical feature which stipulates that these forms undergo Theme Vowel Deletion, in spite of the fact that they do not meet the normal structural description of the rule. The most straightforward way to provide for these irregular applications of Theme Vowel Deletion is to add to Theme Vowel Deletion, a second case which is designated as a Minor Rule. A Minor Rule is one which only applies to segments or forms which are explicitly marked to undergo the rule in question. The revised rule is given as Rule (6.8).

(6.8) Theme Vowel Deletion

$$V \longrightarrow \emptyset \ / \ + \ \underline{\quad} \ + \left\{ \begin{array}{l} \left[\begin{array}{c} V \\ u\ TVD \end{array} \right] \quad \text{(a)} \\ \\ \text{MINOR} \quad \text{(b)} \end{array} \right.$$

6.6.3.2 Athematic future tense forms. A second case of athematicity is the set of irregular future tense forms as analyzed by Harris (1969:96ff.). In Figure 6.12, a set of irregular future tense forms is shown. All manifest absence of the theme vowel. The first four forms in Figure 6.12 can be accounted for solely in terms of irregular application of Theme Vowel Deletion. The next five verbs represented in Figure 6.12 are described in terms of irregular Theme Vowel Deletion plus a D-insertion rule which serves to break up the alveolar sonorant clusters [n r] and [l r]. The final two verbs shown, decir and hacer, require, in addition to irregular Theme Vowel Deletion, a rule which deletes the stem-final consonants. Thus, all the verbs listed in Figure 6.12 must be marked to undergo Theme Vowel Deletion in the future tense.

Figure 6.12. Athematic future stems.

Infinitive	Athematic future stem
haber	habr
querer	querr
poder	podr
saber	sabr
poner	pondr
tener	tendr
venir	vendr
salir	saldr
valer	valdr
decir	dir
hacer	har

Inspection of the list of verbs which undergo irregular Theme Vowel Deletion in the future tense and the list of verbs which have athematic past participles reveals that there is considerable overlapping between the two sets. In fact, throughout the set of irregular verbs in Spanish, it is noted that there is a good deal of overlapping. Once the set of lexical features required for the analysis of irregular verb forms has been determined, a set of redundancy rules must be formulated which expresses these overlappings.

6.6.3.3 Athematic preterite forms. A third instance of athematicity can be seen in the irregular preterite forms. In Figure 6.13, the first and third person singular forms of the irregular preterites are given, along with the infinitive of each verb. The stems of these irregular preterite forms all manifest vowel and consonant alterations which must be specified lexically; and, in addition, the first and third person singular forms have penultimate stress rather than final stress as do the regular preterite forms (cf. [komí] and [komjó]. Since, in addition, the third person singular of the irregular forms lacks the glide [j] which derives from the theme vowel, the most plausible explanation of the stress pattern of the irregular forms is the assumption that the first and third person singular forms are athematic.

However, unlike the future tense, the athematicity of preterite forms does not extend to the entire paradigm; for in [biníste], [binímos] and [binjéron] the theme vowel is present.[10] Thus, it is not possible to mark the verbs which have irregular preterites [+ Theme Vowel Deletion in preterite]. The noteworthy feature of irregular preterite tense forms is that they undergo Theme Vowel Deletion in precisely the context (before a vowel) in which Theme Vowel Deletion normally applies. In fact, regular preterite first and third person singular forms only fail to undergo Theme Vowel Deletion by virtue of the presence of the special exception feature [m TVD],

Figure 6.13. First and third person singular forms of irregular preterites.

Infinitive	First person singular	Third person singular
venir	vine	vino
poder	pude	pudo
poner	puse	puso
saber	supe	supo
caber	cupe	cupo
estar	estuve	estuvo
andar	anduve	anduvo
tener	tuve	tuvo
haber	hube	hubo
traer	traje	trajo
decir	dije	dijo
hacer	hice	hizo
(pro)ducir	(pro)duje	(pro)dujo

which exempts these forms from the rule. Since, from the standpoint of the overall stress pattern of Spanish, penultimate stress is more regular than final stress, it seems quite natural to assume that the 'irregular' aspect of [bíne] and [bíno], etc., consists precisely in the absence of the feature [m TVD] which is associated with the forms [komí] and [komjó]. Thus, the verbs which have irregular preterites should be lexically marked to undergo an erasure of the [m TVD] feature. Derivations for the singular forms of venir are given in Figure 6.14. These derivations assume a lexical entry /ben/ which has features which convert the stem /e/ to /i/ and which trigger the neutralization of the [m TVD] feature.

Figure 6.14. Derivations of singular preterite forms of venir.

	ben+i+i [m TVD]	ben+i+ste	ben+i+u [m TVD]
Stem Change:	i	i	i
Neutralization:	$[u^i$ TVD]		$[u^u$ TVD]
Theme Vowel Deletion:	∅		∅
Stress Assignment:	í	í	í
Lowering	e		o
	[bíne]	[biníste]	[bíno]

6.6.3.4 Athematicity of decir and hacer. A fourth instance of athematicity occurs in the present tense forms of decir and hacer. Since these two verbs have roughly the same derivation, only the forms of decir are cited in this discussion. The present tense forms of decir are the following: [diǥo], [diθes], [diθe], [deθimos], [diθen]. On the surface, the stem-final consonant is manifested as [ǥ] and [θ]. As shown in Section 4.4.2.1, there are good reasons to assume that the underlying form of the stem of this verb is /dik/. The present tense forms lend additional support to this underlying form, because there are phonological rules which convert /k/ to [g] (Lenition) and [θ] (Velar Softening). Furthermore, on the surface, the stem-final /k/ is in the correct environment to yield [g] in [diǥo] and [θ] in [diθe]. An analysis of decir and hacer in terms of these rules was proposed in Foley (1965). His derivations of digo and dice are given in Figure 6.15.

Figure 6.15. Foley's derivations of digo and dice.

	dik + o	dik + e
Velar Softening:	–	θ
Lenition:	g	–
	[diǥo]	[diθe]

However, Foley's analysis is only possible if Theme Vowel Deletion is assumed to precede Velar Softening and Lenition; and Harris (1969:97) has shown that in the derivation of regular verbs, Velar Softening, at least, must precede Theme Vowel Deletion. Otherwise, subjunctive forms of tocar will incorrectly undergo Velar Softening. Correct and incorrect derivations of subjunctive forms of tocar are given in Figure 6.16. Thus, the rule of Velar Softening must precede Theme Vowel Deletion in the regular ordering of these rules.

Figure 6.16. Correct and incorrect derivations of toque.

	tok + a + e
Velar Softening:	–
Theme Vowel Deletion:	∅
	[tóke]

	tok + a + e
Theme Vowel Deletion:	∅
Velar Softening:	θ
	*[toθe]

In spite of these facts brought out by Harris, the phonological processes cited by Foley in his derivations of digo and dice seem correct. The application of Velar Softening to some instances of stem-final /k/ and not to others seems to be conditioned by the vowel which follows this stem in phonetic representations in spite of the fact that this vowel would not follow the stem-final consonant at the point in the derivation when Velar Softening normally applies.

One rather straightforward way of explaining the hard consonant of digo would be to assume that the theme vowel is missing at the point in the derivation when Velar Softening applies to the forms of decir. That is, the usual order of the two rules is reversed, and Theme Vowel Deletion applies to decir before Velar Softening. The derivations of digo and dices are given as Figure 6.17.

Figure 6.17. Derivations of digo and dices.

	dik + e + o	dik + e + s
Theme Vowel Deletion:	Ø	
Velar Softening:	–	θ
Lenition:	g	
	[diǥo]	[diθes]

Note that, in this instance, Theme Vowel Deletion does not apply to any forms other than those to which it would normally apply. The special feature associated with these verbs only changes the ordering of Theme Vowel Deletion so that it applies earlier than it usually does. Thus, it seems that, in addition to exception features which stipulate that a given lexical item undergoes a rule which it should not undergo, another type of lexical exception feature must be postulated which stipulates that, in the case of certain lexical items, the normal order of certain rules is reversed.[11]

6.7 Conclusion. In this chapter, a number of morphological phenomena have been discussed. Spellout rules and rules which define morphological alternations have been formulated. All of these rules apply before the systematic phonemic representation of an utterance, and the distinctions which they introduce are thus considered to be 'phonemic'. The rules are included in this book and in the phonological component because they are essentially concerned with the phonological structure of the forms to which they apply. Thus, it seems it is possible to effect a compromise between the rigid separation of morphology and phonemics attempted by the American structuralists, and the complete obliteration of the distinction between morphological phenomena and phonological phenomena which characterized early work in generative phonology.

NOTES

1. Halle (1973) suggests that the word formation process generates entire paradigms (hablé, hablaste, habló, hablamos, hablasteis, hablaron) which are inserted into syntactic trees. According to Halle's proposal, the correct form is selected later by comparison with the subject. This proposal, however, seems unnecessarily cumbersome. It seems much more reasonable to insert a stem without inflectional endings and allow the correct endings to be spelled out in the morphological subcomponent of the phonology, after the syntactic transformations have specified the agreements upon which inflectional endings sometimes depend.

2. Since Harris (1969) is based upon Mexican Spanish, the vosotros forms, which are not used in Mexico, are not included in his verb paradigms. Harris has provided an analysis of vosotros forms in another paper (Harris (1974c). The analysis of vosotros forms presented in this book is not the same as the analysis presented in Harris (1974c). The reasons for these differences are discussed in Section 6.6.1.2.6.

3. Rule (6.5), for expository purposes only, is formulated so as to apply to a vowel which is specified as [- low]. Technically, since this rule applies in the morphological subcomponent, before the application of the Everywhere Rules, the input should be formulated so as to apply to all vowels which are [u low].

4. It seems likely that the context given in Rule (6.6) is sufficient to restrict the application of the rule to imperfect tense forms. However, if other instances of the sequence . . . i + b . . . are found to exist which do not undergo the rule, then the rule should be reformulated by the addition of features such as [+ past, - perfective] to the context.

5. Harris (1974c) claims that the theme vowel is not deleted from the vosotros forms because at the point in the derivation at which Theme Vowel Deletion applies, the theme vowel of the vosotros forms is followed by a d. However, as explained in Section 6.6.1.2.1, since the publication of Harris' work, it has become clear that the diacritic [u TVD] must be included in the context of Theme Vowel Deletion so that the rule can apply correctly to preterite forms (see Section 6.6.2.4). Thus, one of the main motivations for Harris' rather abstract analysis has vanished. The use of the diacritic [TVD] to explain the failure of the vosotros forms to undergo Theme Vowel Deletion, enables us to assume a much more concrete underlying representation for the vosotros verb endings than does Harris.

6. This stress pattern is irregular if one attempts to maintain a phonetic view of stress, as has consistently been maintained in this book. It should be made clear that this view is not universally held. Hooper (1973), for example, maintains that stress is a systemic feature of the Spanish verb system. Her analysis of the preterite includes the assertion that stress

on the syllable immediately following the stem of the verb is a marker of preterite. Her analysis is plausible because the statement is phonetically accurate as regards the preterite. I have not adopted her view in this matter, because it does not seem that stress has a systemic function in the Spanish verb system as a whole.

7. It should be evident from Bull's comment that the purpose of his book is pedagogical, and not theoretical. Therefore, the 'problems' discussed in connection with his analysis should not be interpreted as a criticism of Bull's work. What is best from a theoretical standpoint and what is most effective pedagogically do not necessarily coincide.

8. In Harris' original analysis, vowels were specified as [+ tense] if Theme Vowel Deletion applied before them, and [- tense] if it did not. As pointed out in Section 6.6.1.2.1, the feature [tense] has been replaced by several diacritics.

9. Other attempts to analyze the preterite forms have been made by Foley (1965) within the generative framework and by Hooper (1973) within the framework of 'natural' generative phonology. An interesting analysis was also presented by Di Pietro (1963) which, although not avowedly generative, included segments which had the power to delete other segments.

10. In the case of [binjéron], the theme vowel is converted to [jé] by the same rule which applies to regular forms such as [komjéron].

11. The suggestion that the order of two rules can be reversed in the case of particular lexical items is interesting in relation to a theory of Local Ordering proposed in Anderson (1970:394ff.). For a complete discussion of how Anderson's Local Ordering theory relates to the derivations of decir and hacer, see Cressey (1972).

APPENDIX

DESCRIPTION OF THE PRINCIPAL SOUNDS OF SPANISH IN TERMS OF THE IPA CLASSIFICATION SYSTEM

A.0 Introduction. In the sections which follow, descriptions of the principal sounds of Spanish are given in terms of the classification system developed by the International Phonetic Association (see International Phonetic Association 1949) which consists of specifications of point of articulation, manner of articulation, and voicing. In most cases a comparison with English sounds which are identical or similar is also given. For a fuller account of the exact articulation and the environments of each sound, the reader is referred to Navarro Tomás (1968).

A.1 Vowel sounds

A.1.1 General characteristics of Spanish vowels. All Spanish vowels are shorter, tenser, and somewhat higher than their English stressed counterparts. On the other hand, Spanish unstressed vowels are not shortened as much as are English unstressed vowels. In other words, Spanish stressed vowels are shorter than English stressed vowels, and Spanish unstressed vowels are longer than English unstressed vowels.

These two phenomena are related to each other and are the result of differing rhythm patterns in the two languages. English is 'stress timed', which means that each group of syllables containing one stressed vowel has approximately the same duration regardless of the total number of syllables in the group. Spanish, on the other hand, is 'syllable timed', which means that every syllable has approximately the same duration regardless of whether its vowel is stressed or unstressed. This difference in timing is what causes English stressed vowels to be diphthongized and English unstressed vowels to be reduced to schwa([ə]), a mid center vowel as in 'an apple'. This difference is probably also what accounts for the difference in the way of calculating the metre of English and Spanish poetry. In English poetry, the number of 'feet' is counted, and each foot contains one stressed vowel (two lines are deemed to be of equal length if they contain an equal number of feet), whereas in Spanish poetry all syllables (stressed and unstressed) are counted in order to determine the metre. Thus the difference in calculating is based, not upon an arbitrary convention, but on a feature of the two languages.

A.1.2 The five principal Spanish vowels. Vowels are commonly displayed in a triangular arrangement which indicates the position of the body of the tongue in the articulation of each. In the articulation of vowels near the top of the triangle, the body of the tongue is raised, and in the articulation of vowels near the bottom, the tongue is lowered. In the articulation of vowels on the right-hand side of the triangle, the tongue is held in a forward position; in the articulation of those on the left side, it is held in a back position. In Figure A.1, the five principal Spanish vowels are shown using the triangle arrangement.

Figure A.1.   Triangle display of the five principal vowels of Spanish.

```
u            i
    o    e
       a
```

A.1.2.1 Descriptions. In each of the descriptions which follow, the phonetic symbol which represents the sound is given between square brackets ([a]); the way or ways of spelling the sound in the standard orthography is given underlined (a), some examples of words containing the sound are given, and the position of the body of the tongue is specified (it is either 'front', 'central', or 'back' and it is either 'high', 'mid', or 'low'). In addition, some equivalent sounds in English are given, if possible.

A.1.2.1.1 [u] orth: u; tú, su. High back vowel. The most similar sound in English is the vowel sound of boo! (as if to scare someone). That is, the Spanish sound is shorter, somewhat tenser, and somewhat higher than the English sound of two, Sue, etc. These English words have vocalic elements which are best characterized as composed of two segments--a vowel followed by a glide: [tuʷ] [suʷ]. Although this compound quality is common to most English stressed vowels, it is completely lacking in Spanish.

A.1.2.1.2 [o] orth: o; lo, no. Mid back vowel. Similar to the English vowel of no, low; however, as in the case of [u], the Spanish vowel is articulated without the glide element present in English.

Spanish   English

lo [lo]   low [loʷ]
no [no]   no [noʷ]

A.1.2.1.3 [a] orth: a; la, ha. Low central vowel. Similar to English a in father.

A.1.2.1.4 [e] orth: e; he, te. Mid front vowel. Similar to the English vowel in bay, say but without the glide element.

A.1.2.1.5 [i] orth: i, y; y, ti, si. High front vowel. Similar to English ee in see.

A.1.3 Vowel variants

A.1.3.1 Lowered mid and high vowels

A.1.3.1.1 [ǫ] orth: o; con, son. Low mid back vowel. There are so many dialect differences with respect to English sounds which are similar to Spanish [ǫ], that it is difficult to suggest an approximation. For standard 'radio' English, at least, Spanish [ǫ] is about midway between the vowel sounds of pawn and pun. However, this is not true for dialects which tend to 'emphasize the w' of pawn, nor for those which pronounce aw as ah.

A.1.3.1.2 [ę] orth: e; el, ver. Low-mid front vowel. Quite similar to English e in ten, Ben; perhaps a bit higher.

A.1.3.1.3 [ʉ] orth: u; turco, insulto. Lowered high back vowel. Articulation of this sound is slightly lower than than of [u], but not as low as the articulation of English u of put.

A.1.3.1.4 [i̢] orth: i; gentil, virtud. Lowered high front vowel. Articulation of this sound is slightly lower than [i], but not as low as that of English i in think.

A.1.3.2 Variants of [a]

A.1.3.2.1 [ạ] orth: a; mal, bajo. Velarized low central vowel. Articulation of this sound is slightly higher, and slightly posterior of the articulation of [a].

A.1.3.2.2 [ą] orth: a; macho, calle. Palatalized low central vowel. Articulation of this sound is slightly higher and slightly to the front of that of [a]. It is not fronted as much as the a of English cat.

A.1.3.3 Relaxed vowels. Corresponding to each of the five principal vowel sounds, there is a 'relaxed' vowel, which is shorter, less tense, and articulated with less precision than their nonrelaxed counterparts. The symbols are [ʊ ɔ ɐ ə ɪ]

A.2 Glides. The distinction between on-glides (before a vowel in the same syllable) and off-glides (after a vowel in the same syllable) is not represented using separate symbols in this book (see Section 1.2.3.1). In addition to the principal glides defined in the sections which follow, nonhigh glides have been defined in Section 1.2.3.2.

A.2.1 [w] orth: u; deuda, bueno. Back glide. When an unstressed u follows another vowel, it is pronounced as a glide rather than as a full vowel. The sound is similar (but somewhat higher and shorter) to the glide in English loud. When an unstressed u precedes another vowel and is preceded by a consonant, it is pronounced as a glide similar to the u of English queer or the w of wall.

A.2.2 [j] orth: i, y; bien, veinte, rey. Front glide. When an unstressed i (sometimes y) follows another vowel, it is pronounced as a glide. The sound is similar to the glide in English say, but, as in the case of [w], somewhat higher and shorter. When an unstressed i precedes another vowel and is preceded by a consonant, it is pronounced as a glide similar to English y as in yet.

A.3 Consonants

A.3.1 The IPA classification system

A.3.1.1 Points of articulation for Spanish. The point of articulation describes the point in the mouth at which the primary obstruction is located.

bilabial: the two lips
labio-dental: the lower lip and the upper teeth
interdental: the tip of the tongue and the cutting edge
   of the upper teeth
dental: the tip of the tongue and the back of the upper
   teeth
alveolar: the tip of the tongue and the gum ridge immediately behind the upper teeth
palato-alveolar: the tip of the tongue and the hard area
   just behind the gums

palatal: the body of the tongue and the roof of the
mouth
velar: the body of the tongue and the very back part
of the roof of the mouth.

A.3.1.2 Manners of articulation for Spanish. The following
terms describe the type of obstruction which is present in the
articulation of the sound.

stop: the speech canal is closed off completely, causing
an interruption in the air flow.
fricative: complete closure is not made, but the speech
organs are brought into close proximity causing friction
affricate: complete closure is made causing a stop, but
the release is gradual causing friction
nasal: the nasal tract is opened during articulation
allowing air to escape through the nose
lateral: the sides of the tongue are lowered during
articulation, allowing air to escape along the sides of
the mouth.
vibrant: (flap, trill):   the tip of the tongue is brought
into close proximity with the gums, and the Bernoulli
effect (loss of pressure due to the increased speed of
the air flow) causes the tongue to make contact with
the gums once or more.
sibilant: the tongue directs the air flow against the
teeth producing a hissing noise.

A.3.1.3 Voicing. Voiced sounds are produced with vibrations in the glottis (English z, n, l, b, etc.); voiceless
sounds are produced without such vibrations (English s, p,
f, sh, ch, etc.).

A.3.2 IPA display of Spanish consonants. These three
characteristics of consonants have been used to classify the
consonants of Spanish as represented in Figure A.2. Manner
of articulation is listed on the left side, point of articulation
across the top, and voicing is represented by a left (voiceless)
versus right (voiced) dimension within each box. The principal consonants of Spanish are displayed using this characteriza-
tion system in Figure A.2.

A.3.3 Descriptions. In the sections that follow, the sounds
corresponding to the phonetic symbols used in Figure A.2 are
described, related to Spanish orthography, and related to English sounds.

A.3.3.1 Stops

A.3.3.1.1 [p]   orth: p; pan, apto.   Voiceless bilabial stop.

Figure A.2. IPA display of principal Spanish consonants.

	bilabial	labio-dental	interdental	dental	alveolar	palato-alveolar	palatal	velar
stops	p b			t d				k g
fricatives	ƀ	f	θ z̦	đ			y	x ǥ
affricates						č	ŷ	
nasals	m	m̦	n̦	ņ	n	ɦ	ñ	ŋ
laterals			ḷ	ḽ	l	ḽ	l̃	
vibrants					r r̃			
sibilants				ș z̧		s	z	

Spanish [p] differs from English p in that it is not aspirated (followed by a puff of air) as is English p in certain environments:

Aspirated English p: [p'ɨn]
Unaspirated English p: [spɨn]
Unaspirated Spanish p: [pan]

A.3.3.1.2 [b] orth: b, v; vamos, ambos. Voiced bilabial stop. Substantially equivalent to English b in boy.

A.3.3.1.3 [t] orth: t; todo, gato. Voiceless dental stop. Spanish [t] differs from English t in two ways: like [p] it is always unaspirated, and Spanish [t] is dental, whereas English t is alveolar.

A.3.3.1.4 [d] orth: d; démelo, ando, Donaldo. Voiced dental stop. Differs in point of articulation from English (alveolar) d.

A.3.3.1.5 [k] orth: c, k, q; caballo, kilo, que. Voiceless velar stop. Differs from English k in that it is unaspirated.

A.3.3.1.6 [g] orth: g; gato, ángulo. Voiced velar stop. Substantially equivalent to English g as in get.

A.3.3.2 Fricatives

A.3.3.2.1 [ƀ] orth: b, v; haber, alba, esbelto. Voiced bilabial fricative. This sound differs from English v in that it is bilabial, whereas the English v is labio-dental.

A.3.3.2.2 [f] orth: f, familia, afán. Voiceless labio-dental fricative. Substantially equivalent to English f.

A.3.3.2.3 [θ] orth: c, z; cine, voz. Voiceless interdental fricative. Substantially equivalent to English th as in think.

A.3.3.2.4 [đ] orth: d; cada, Madrid. Voiced dental fricative. This sound is somewhat similar to English th as in those. However, unlike the English sound, Spanish [đ] has the same point of articulation as [d] (i.e. it is dental rather than interdental).

A.3.3.2.5 [y] orth: y, hi (ll in some dialects), ayer, hierba. Voiced palatal fricative. This sound is articulated with much more friction than English y and differs from English s of pleasure in that it is articulated without the retroflexion (curling up of the tongue) which characterizes this English sound.

A.3.3.2.6 [x] orth: j, g; jamón, gente. Voiceless velar fricative. There is no equivalent English sound. The sound is produced with a great deal more friction than English h.

A.3.3.2.7 [ǥ] orth: g; lago, traigo. Voiced velar fricative. No English equivalent.

A.3.3.3 Affricates

A.3.3.3.1 [ĉ] orth: ch; chico, ponche. Voiceless palato-alveolar fricative. Substantially equivalent to English ch.

A.3.3.3.2 [ŷ] orth: y, ll, hi (in some dialects); conyuge, el hielo, yo. Voiced palatal fricative. This sound is similar to English g of George. However, as in the case of [y], the Spanish sound is articulated without retroflexion.

A.3.3.4 Nasals

A.3.3.4.1 Principal nasal sounds

A.3.3.4.1.1 [m] orth: m; cama, mi. Voiced bilabial nasal. Substantially equivalent to English m.

A.3.3.4.1.2 [n] orth: n; cana, ni. Voiced alveolar nasal. Substantially equivalent to English n.

A.3.3.4.1.3 [ñ] orth: ñ; caña. Voiced palatal nasal. Substantially equivalent to English ny as in canyon.

A.3.4.2 Variants of nasals. Due to assimilation of Spanish nasals to a following consonant, there is a nasal consonant at each point of articulation, as shown in Figure A.3.

Figure A.3. Nasal consonants of Spanish.

[m] : [um beso]	bilabial
[m̜] : [um̜ fenomeno]	labio-dental
[n̪] : [un̪ apato]	interdental
[n̺] : [un̺ dia]	dental
[n] : [un niño]	alveolar
[ñ] : [uñ ĉiko]	palato-alveolar
[ñ] : [uñ ñandu]	palatal
[ŋ] : [uŋ gato]	velar

A.3.3.5 Laterals

A.3.3.5.1 Principal laterals

A.3.3.5.1.1 [l] orth: l; ola, lápiz, algo. Voiced alveolar lateral. Similar to English l in leak. Unlike English l (e.g. in

Bill, gull) Spanish [l] is always 'i-colored' (i.e. pronounced with the body of the tongue high and forward as for [i]).

A.3.3.5.1.2 [ĺ] orth: ll; calle, llave. Voiced palatal lateral. Substantially equivalent to English li as in Castilian.

A.3.3.5.2 **Variants of laterals.** Before inter-dental, dental, and palato-alveolar consonants, l takes on the point of articulation of the consonant which follows; as shown in Figure A.4.

Figure A.4. Lateral consonants of Spanish.

[ḷ]	: [aḷθar]	inter-dental
[ḷ]	: [aḷto]	dental
[l]	: [el niđo]	alveolar
[ĺ]	: [èl ĉiko]	palato-alveolar
[ĩ]	: [el̃ ĩaƀero]	palatal

A.3.3.6 **Vibrants**

A.3.3.6.1 [r] orth: r; pero, trabajo. Simple (flap) voiced vibrant. Similar to English tt as in letter (if pronounced rapidly).

A.3.3.6.2 [r̃] orth: r, rr; perro, rey. Multiple (trill) voiced vibrant. No equivalent in English.

A.3.3.7 **Sibilants.** The dialect described in this book is that of Castile, and most of the northern part of Spain. In this dialect, s has a point of articulation which is considerably further back in the mouth than the point of articulation of English s. (See Navarro Tomás 1968:105ff.) This sibilant is subject to two assimilatory processes: it becomes voiced if followed by a voiced consonant, and it becomes dental if followed by a dental consonant.

A.3.3.7.1 [s] orth: s; casa, asco. Voiceless palato-alveolar sibilant. This sound is produced with the tongue in a retroflex position similar to that of [ĉ] (perhaps somewhat further back with the tip of the tongue pointing straight up, and with the body of the tongue held low).

A.3.3.7.2 [z] orth: s; mismo, asno. Voiced palato-alveolar sibilant. This is the voiced equivalent of [s].

A.3.3.7.3 [ş] orth: s; este, escena. Voiceless dental sibilant.

A.3.3.7.4 [ʐ] orth: s; desde. Voiced dental sibilant.

REFERENCES

Alarcos Llorach, Emilio. 1968. Fonología española. Madrid:
Editorial Gredos.

Anderson, Stephen R. 1970. On Grassman's law in Sanskrit.
Linguistic Inquiry 1.387-396.

Anderson, Stephen R. 1974. The organization of phonology.
New York: Academic Press.

Aronoff, Mark. 1976. Word formation in generative grammar.
Cambridge, Massachusetts: MIT Press.

Bailey, Charles-James N. 1972. Variation and linguistic
theory. Unpublished manuscript, Georgetown University.

Bowen, J. Donald, and R. P. Stockwell. 1955. The phonemic
interpretation of semivowels in Spanish. Lg. 31.236-240.

Bowen, J. Donald, and R. P. Stockwell. 1956. A further note
on Spanish semivowels. Lg. 32.290-292.

Boyd-Bowman, Peter. 1954. From Latin to Romance in sound
charts. Kalamazoo, Michigan: Kalamazoo College.

Brame, M. K., and Ivonne Bordelois. 1973. Vocalic alternations in Spanish. Linguistic Inquiry 4.111-168.

Bull, William. 1965. Spanish for teachers. New York: Ronald
Press.

Cedergren, Henrietta. 1973. The interplay of social and linguistic factors in Panama. Unpublished Ph.D. dissertation.

Chavarría-Aguilar, O. L. 1951. The phonemes of Costa Rican
Spanish. Lg. 27.248-253.

Chomsky, Noam. 1964. Current issues in linguistic theory.
In: Fodor and Katz (1964).

Chomsky, Noam. 1965. Aspects of the theory of syntax.
Cambridge, Massachusetts: MIT Press.

Chomsky, Noam, and Morris Halle. 1968. The sound pattern
of English. New York: Harper and Row.

Contreras, Heles. 1969. Simplicity, descriptive adequacy, and
binary features. Lg. 45.1-8.

Cressey, William. 1968. Relative adverbs in Spanish. Lg.
44.487-500.

161

Cressey, William. 1970a. Two proposed conditions governing
phonological theory. Paper read at the Annual Meeting of
the Linguistic Society of America, Washington, D.C.

Cressey, William. 1970b. A note on specious simplification
and the theory of markedness. Papers in Linguistics 2.227-
237.

Cressey, William. 1971. Review of: Harris (1969). General
Linguistics 11.63-70.

Cressey, William. 1972. Irregular verbs in Spanish. In:
Generative studies in Romance languages. Edited by Casagrande and Saciuk. Rowley, Massachusetts: Newbury House.

Dinnsen, Daniel. 1974. The fallacy of strict sequentiality.
Bloomington: Indiana University Linguistics Club.

Di Pietro, Robert J. 1963. Morphemic analysis of the Spanish
verb. Filología Moderna 13.53-58.

Elcock, W. D. 1960. The Romance languages. London:
Faber and Faber.

Fodor and Katz, eds. 1964. The structure of language.
Englewood Cliffs, New Jersey: Prentice-Hall.

Foley, James. 1965. Spanish morphology. Unpublished Ph.D.
dissertation, Massachusetts Institute of Technology.

Foley, James A. 1969. Phonological distinctive features.
Paper read at the 44th Annual Meeting of the Linguistic
Society of America.

Foley, James A. 1972. Assibilation in Spanish first singular
verb forms: Interrupted rule schemata. In: Generative
studies in Romance languages. Edited by Casagrande and
Saciuk. Rowley, Massachusetts: Newbury House.

Friedman, Joyce, and Yves-Charles Morin. 1971. Phonological
grammar tester: Description. Ann Arbor, Michigan: The
University of Michigan Phonetics Laboratory.

Fromkin, Victoria. 1971. A reply to P. Ladefogged's The
phonetic framework of generative phonology. Unpublished
manuscript, University of Michigan.

Guitart, Jorge M. 1976. Markedness and a Cuban dialect of
Spanish. Washington, D.C.: Georgetown University Press.

Halle, Morris. 1973. Prolegomena to a theory of word formation. Linguistic Inquiry 4.3-16.

Harms, Robert T. 1968. Introduction to phonological theory.
Englewood Cliffs, New Jersey: Prentice-Hall.

Harris, James W. 1969. Spanish phonology. Cambridge,
Massachusetts: MIT Press.

Harris, James W. 1970. Sequences of vowels in Spanish.
Linguistic Inquiry 1.129-134.

Harris, James W. 1974a. Morphologization of phonological
rules: An example from Chicano Spanish. In: Linguistic
studies in Romance languages. Edited by Campbell, et al.
Washington, D.C.: Georgetown University Press.

Harris, James W. 1974b. Stress assignment rules in Spanish.
In: Current studies in Romance linguistics. Edited by Luján
and Hensey. Washington, D.C.: Georgetown University Press.

Harris, James. 1974c. Las formas verbales de segunda persona plural y otras cuestiones de fonología y morfología. Revista de lingüística aplicada y teórica. Universidad de Concepción, Chile.

Hooper, Joan. 1972. The syllable in phonological theory. Lg. 48.525-540.

Hooper, Joan. 1976. An introduction to natural generative phonology. New York: Academic Press.

Hooper, Joan, and Tracy Terrell. 1976. Stress assignment in Spanish: A natural generative analysis. Glossa 10.64-110.

International Phonetic Association. 1949. The principles of the International Phonetic Association. London, England: Department of Phonetics, University College.

Jacobson, R., G. Fant, and M. Halle. 1963. Preliminaries to speech analysis. Cambridge, Massachusetts: MIT Press.

Kim, C.-W. 1965. On the autonomy of the tensity feature in stop classification. Word 21.339-359.

King, H. V. 1952. Outline of Mexican Spanish phonology. Studies in Linguistics 10.51-62.

Kiparsky, Paul. 1968a. How abstract is phonology? Bloomington: Indiana University Linguistics Club.

Kiparsky, Paul. 1968b. Linguistic universals and linguistic change. In: Universals in linguistic theory. Edited by Bach and Harms. New York: Holt, Rinehart and Winston.

Labov, William. 1966. The social stratification of English in New York City. Washington, D.C.: Center for Applied Linguistics.

Ladefogged, Peter. 1971. The phonetic framework of generative phonology. Unpublished manuscript, University of Michigan.

Lakoff, George. 1971. On generative semantics. In: Semantics. Edited by Steinberg and Jacobovitz. Cambridge, England: Cambridge University Press.

Lapesa, Rafael. 1959. Historia de la lengua española. New York: Las Américas.

Lightner, T. M. 1963. A note on the formulation of phonological rules. Quarterly Progress Report of the Research Laboratory of Electronics, Massachusetts Institute of Technology.

Lisker, L., and A. Abramson. 1964. A cross-language study of voicing in initial stops: Acoustical measurements. Word 20.384-422.

Lisker, L., and A. Abramson. 1971. Distinctive features and laryngeal control. Lg. 47.767-785.

Menéndez Pidal, Ramón. 1950. Orígenes del español. Madrid: Espasa-Calpe.

Mey, Jacob. 1970. Mark and switch. Papers in Linguistics 2.503-521.

Morin, Yves-Charles, and Joyce Friedman. 1971. Phonological grammar tester: Underlying theory. Ann Arbor, Michigan: The University of Michigan Phonetics Laboratory.

Navarro Tomás, Tomás. 1968. Manual de pronunciación española. Madrid: Consejo Superior de Investigaciones Científicas.

Postal, Paul. 1968. Aspects of phonological theory. New York: Harper and Row.

Quilis, Antonio, and Joseph Fernandez. 1969. Curso de fonética y fonología españolas. Madrid: Consejo Superior de Investigaciones Científicas.

Ramsey, Marathon Montrose. 1894. A textbook of modern Spanish. New York: Holt, Rinehart and Winston.

Real Academia Española. 1885. Ortografía de la lengua castellana. Madrid: Imprensa Real.

Saciuk, Bohdan. 1974. Spanish stress and language change. In: Linguistic studies in Romance languages. Edited by Campbell, et al. Washington, D.C.: Georgetown University Press.

Saporta, Sol. 1959. Morpheme alternants in Spanish. In: Structural studies on Spanish themes. Edited by: Kahane and Pietrangeli. Salamanca: Acta Salamanticensia.

Saporta, Sol. 1956. A note on Spanish semivowels. Lg. 32.287-290.

Silva-Fuenzalida, I. 1952. Estudio fonológico del español de Chile. Boletín de filología 7.153-176.

Spaulding, Robert. 1962. How Spanish grew. Berkeley, California: University of California Press.

Stockwell, R. P., J. D. Bowen, and J. W. Martin. 1965. The grammatical structures of English and Spanish. Chicago: University of Chicago Press.

Trager, G. L. 1939. The phonemes of Castilian Spanish. Travaux du Cercle Linguistique de Prague 8.217-222.

INDEX

α See: alpha notation
< > See: angled parentheses
<> See: large angled parentheses
+ See: morpheme boundary
| | See: phonetic phrase boundary
− See: syllable boundary
See: word boundary

abbreviatory devices 2.5, 3.1.1.2
abstract phonological feature See: diacritic
abstractness 0.1.2, 2.1, 2.9, 4.2
adequacy 0.4
allomorph 0.4, 3.1.1.1, 6.0
allophonic process 3.0
alpha notation 1.2.2.3.2, 3.1.1.2, 3.2.3.1
alpha [PA] 3.1.1.2
American structural linguistics 0.1.1, 2.2, 4.6.2, 6.0, 6.6.2
angled parentheses 3.3; See also: large angled parentheses
[anterior] 1.2.4.1.2.1, 5.6.4
assimilation 3.1, 3.3, 4.8
athematicity 6.6.3
autonomous phonemics 2.2

[back] 1.2.2.2.3, 1.2.4.1.1, 5.6.4
Bernoulli effect 1.2.5.2.3
binary feature 5.6.2
bi-uniqueness condition 3.1.1.1
blade of the tongue 1.2.4.1.2
boundaries 4.2.1.3
braces 2.5
broad phonetic representation 1.1.3

C 1.2.1.2
Castilian s̱ Figure 1.16
classical g̅rammarians 0.1.2

165